THE YOUNG ADVENTURER'S GUIDE TO (ALMOST) EVERYTHING

THE YOUNG ADVENTURER'S GUIDE TO (ALMOST) EVERYTHING

BUILD A FORT, CAMP LIKE A CHAMP,
POOP IN THE WOODS—
45 ACTION-PACKED OUTDOOR ACTIVITIES

BEN AND **PENNY HEWITT**

ILLUSTRATIONS BY LUKE BOUSHEE

ROOST BOOKS
BOULDER 2019

ROOST BOOKS
An imprint of Shambhala Publications, Inc.
2129 13th Street
Boulder, Colorado 80302
roostbooks.com

9 8 7 6 5

Printed in Malaysia

Shambhala Publications makes every effort to print on acid-free,
recycled paper.

Roost Books is distributed worldwide by Penguin Random House, Inc.,
and its subsidiaries.

Designed by Liz Quan

LIBRARY OF CONGRESS
CATALOGING-IN-PUBLICATION DATA
Names: Hewitt, Ben, 1971– author. | Hewitt, Penny, author. |
    Boushee, Luke, illustrator.
Title: The young adventurer's guide to (almost) everything: build a fort,
    camp like a champ, poop in the woods—45 action-packed outdoor
    activities/Ben and Penny Hewitt; illustrations by Luke Boushee.
Description: First Edition. | Boulder: Roost Books, 2019. | Audience: Age
    8–12
Identifiers: LCCN 2018013405 | ISBN 9781611805949 (hardcover: alk.
    paper)
Subjects: LCSH: Outdoor recreation for children—Juvenile literature. |
    Nature study—Activity programs—Juvenile literature.
Classification: LCC GV191.63 .H48 2019 | DDC 796.083—dc23
LC record available at https://lccn.loc.gov/2018013405

CONTENTS

PART TWO

THE BEST CAMPING TRIP EVER

PART THREE

MAKE REALLY COOL STUFF THAT'S ACTUALLY USEFUL

PART FOUR

TURN THE ORDINARY INTO THE EXTRAORDINARY

INTRODUCTION

➤━━━━━━━➤

ONCE UPON A TIME, people learned the most awesome and useful things. They learned how to find wild food in the fields and forests, how to shelter themselves with nothing more than sticks and leaves, how to maintain a knife and hatchet, even how to build a fire without matches or a lighter. They learned these skills from those who came before them, and they passed them along to those who came after. It was just the way the world worked.

People learned how to do these things because if they didn't, they died. That's not quite how it is today: these days, we're more likely to fear losing our Wi-Fi signal than getting lost in the woods. Of course, technology and the evolution of human knowledge have brought amazing things into our lives. Despite the so-called primitive nature of many of the skills in this book, we don't believe that humans should return to living in caves, and we don't believe that new technologies are inherently bad. Rather, we believe that technologies old and new can be used in ways that are both productive and destructive. For instance, a stone can be used to grind acorns into flour, or it can be used to thump someone over the head. Likewise, a smartphone can be used to share things of beauty and importance, or it can be used to spread messages of hate and intolerance. It's the same stone, the same phone; only the intention is different.

We also believe that keeping the skills in this book alive is critical to maintaining our connection to nature, and that right now, in an era of rapid climate change and the ongoing loss of wild places and creatures, this connection is more important than ever. Because if we don't feel connected, it's hard for us to truly care. Learning and practicing these skills isn't merely about what the skills can do for you—the food you'll learn to forage and process, or the medicine you'll learn to make, or even the games you'll learn to play. Don't get us wrong: that's all well and good and fun—and fun is a big part of what this book is about. But there is more to it than that.

Many of the skills depicted in this book originated with Native Americans, the first inhabitants of North America. Indeed, many are still practiced by these people. While it's common to think of Native Americans as being part of the past, in fact there are currently well over five hundred tribes in the United States, comprising more than five million members. And this number doesn't even begin to account for everyone in the United States who has some percentage of indigenous blood running through them.

As direct descendants of the people who wrongfully took control of the land we now call "ours," it is difficult to know how to properly acknowledge and honor the contributions and cultures of native peoples. We feel deep respect and love for the people, cultures, and ways of living that are directly connected to the Earth. Often, the true masters of these ways have been indigenous peoples; we are grateful for the opportunity to learn their ways, and we draw tremendous inspiration from their practices.

"TRUTH IS, IF THE ONLY REASON YOU PICKED UP THIS BOOK IS BECAUSE YOU WANT TO FREAK OUT YOUR PARENTS BY COOKING UP A BATCH OF FRIED GRASSHOPPERS, THAT'S OK, TOO."

There is a fine line between learning from native people (and keeping these skills alive) and what is known as "cultural appropriation," which is adopting certain elements of a particular culture without express permission. That line can sometimes be uncertain; the important thing is to be aware that these issues exist and to work at deepening our understanding of them. And don't be afraid to ask questions. As long as you approach people with respect and humility, there is no such thing as a wrong question; there are only wrong assumptions.

The late American philosopher Alan Bloom once wrote, "We need history, not to tell us what happened, or to explain the past, but to make the past alive so that it can explain us and make a future possible." That connection to the past and future is part of why we believe these skills are important.

That's a lot to think about, and if it doesn't resonate with you, that's OK. Truth is, if the only reason you picked up this book is because you think it'd be cool to spend a night in a shelter made from sticks, or because you want to freak out your parents by cooking up a batch of fried grasshoppers, that's OK, too. There's no right or wrong way to use this book.

The skills on the following pages cover a wide range of difficulty. Some of them you can tackle alone, and some might require the help of a parent or friend with a bit more experience than yourself. Don't be shy about asking for help; a big part of the fun is working on these projects with others, sharing in the mistakes and the triumphs, finding solutions together, and creating a sense of community around working with wild materials. And chances are, if it's one or both of your parents you're working with, you might be able to teach them a thing or two.

Finally, we would like to extend our immense gratitude to the friends and teachers who have given freely of their time to share these skills with us.

Now, turn the pages and start exploring!

THE SAFE AND HONORABLE HARVEST

———▶———

When it comes to determining the ethics of harvesting wild foods and other resources, we can do no better than to share Robin Wall Kimmerer's Honorable Harvest guidelines from her excellent book *Braiding Sweetgrass: Indigenous Wisdom, Scientific Knowledge, and the Teachings of Plants.* They look like this:

Ask permission of the ones whose lives you seek. Abide by the answer.

Never take the first. Never take the last.

Harvest in a way that minimizes harm.

Take only what you need and leave some for others.

Use everything that you take.

Take only that which is given to you.

Share it, as the Earth has shared with you.

Be grateful.

Reciprocate the gift.

Sustain the ones who sustain you, and the Earth will last forever.

Of course, there are other considerations not directly related to ethics. Chief among them is ensuring that you've properly identified the plants you're about to harvest. A good rule of thumb is to confirm your identification with three sources. We're particularly fond of Samuel Thayer's books *The Forager's Harvest* and *Nature's Garden*, although, if possible, it's always best if at least one source is a real-live human being!

One other thing: Always be certain that the edible plants you're about to harvest have not been subject to herbicides or pesticides that can be dangerous to your health. This is of particular concern in maintained public areas such as city parks, where spraying is common. If you don't know, don't eat!

CHOOSING A KNIFE AND HANDLING IT SAFELY

THE MOST IMPORTANT TOOL YOU'LL OWN

IT WASN'T SO LONG AGO that most kids were given a knife at some point before their tenth birthday, taught how to use and care for it, and, perhaps most importantly, were trusted with it. In many instances, this was the same knife a child's parent or grandparent had used, and handing it down across the generations was part of the family's legacy.

Of course, these days most kids don't live on farms or even in the country, and the need for children—or adults, for that matter—to carry a sharp cutting implement isn't what it was. Until you opened this book, that is, because as you flip through these pages, you'll find more uses for a knife than you can shake a stick at.

CHOOSING

FIXED BLADES

Most people think of a pocketknife as the best knife for a kid, but truth is, the safest, most useful knife is one with a fixed blade in a belt sheath. Thanks to its lack of moving parts, a fixed-blade knife does not fold or slide and is typically stronger due to the tang, which is the extension of the blade into the handle. With a fixed-blade knife, there is no chance of it folding on your fingers when you least expect it. As a bonus, these knives are usually more comfortable to hold and work with.

We get most of our knives from Ragweed Forge, through the website www.ragweedforge.com, and especially recommend the Mora knives made in Sweden. They are made with Swedish steel and skilled craftsmanship and are the best bang for your buck around. They are simple and easy to sharpen (although they come from the factory very sharp). For fourteen bucks, you can get one of the "Classic Mora" knives, which comes with a plastic sheath that goes on your belt and will last you a lifetime (if you don't lose it!). The site also offers more expensive leather sheath options, or you can, of course, make your own sheath (see page 126). If you are new to using knives, the Classic Mora can be purchased in a version with a blade guard so your hand cannot slip down the handle onto the blade.

If you think you will be mostly carving with your knife, look in the wood-carving section of the Mora catalog and you will find #106, a knife that is narrower and pointed and our favorite for that purpose.

Lastly, Ragnar at Ragweed Forge is super accommodating and happy to answer questions, so don't be shy.

FOLDING POCKETKNIVES

We know that no matter what we say here, some of you will disregard the sage advice of your elders and get yourselves a pocketknife. That's OK, you're young; every so often, you're *supposed* to disregard the sage advice of your elders. Here's what we recommend when it comes to pocketknives:

LOCKING BLADE. Don't get a knife without it. These knives have a mechanism that locks the blade in its fully opened position. The lock must be released before the knife can be folded, eliminating accidental closures.

QUALITY. Don't get a cheap junker. It seems like you've gotta throw down at least thirty bucks for anything decent, and the $35 to $65 range has a heck of a lot more options.

SIMPLICITY. Get a single midsized blade. Big and small blades are harder to control and less versatile. Those pocketknives with all kinds of gadgets that try to prepare you for the zombie apocalypse always compromise on something—if you don't lose comfort in the hand, you might end up with enough weight to drag your pants down around your ankles.

Not to beat a dead horse, but a fixed blade solves all those issues, no muss, no fuss. Don't say we didn't warn ya!

HOOK KNIVES

A hook knife is a specialty carving tool used for hollowing out bowls or creating spoons. Unfortunately, the ones on the Ragweed Forge website made by Mora (who we love, love, love for carving and general-purpose knives) are not that great. Go to the websites of Pinewood Forge (www.pinewoodforge.com), Deepwoods Ventures (www.deepwoodsventures.com), or Wood Tools (www.woodtools.co.uk) to find a quality hook knife, or show a local blacksmith those sites and get one made just for you.

HANDLING

These safety tips may seem like common sense, but sometimes common sense isn't as common as it should be!

▶ A knife is a tool; use it accordingly.

▶ When using a knife, do not stand or sit within one and a half arm lengths of anyone in any direction. This is considered your "circle of blood." Anyone coming within this circle is at risk of getting cut. It is the knife user's responsibility to maintain this circle.

▶ When passing an open knife to someone, offer the butt end of the handle. Make sure the spine of the knife blade is toward your palm with the blade facing away from your skin.

▶ Do not carve anything that does not belong to you or for which you do not have permission to carve. This includes trees, bathroom doors, and picnic tables!

▶ With some techniques, you can safely carve toward yourself—but when you are starting out, whittle away from your body.

▶ Do not carve toward your leg, knee, a table, or any other object. Spread your knees and carve directly between your spread legs or toward the outside of your leg.

▶ Keep your knife clean and sharp.

SHARPENING

A sharp tool is a safe tool. This goes for knives, axes, gouges, or anything with a cutting edge. Compensating for a dull blade by applying force can cause serious injuries. If the knife blade is suddenly freed from the cut, the momentum can cause a loss of control.

There are as many takes on blade sharpening as there are people who sharpen blades, and most of them work. People seem to stick to the technique and the sharpening stone they were taught on. Most hand skills are easiest to learn from someone who is accomplished at the skill, but with knife sharpening, multiply that truth by ten. Seek out an old-timer, a woodworker, a butcher, or anyone else who uses knives regularly or just seems like one of those folks who knows useful stuff.

Short of finding a teacher, buy a sharpening stone and read the directions. Beginners should start with diamond stones. Not only are diamond stones low maintenance and durable, but they are also considered the fastest to use. Roughly 8 inches by 2½ inches is a good size. You will need a coarse and a fine-grit stone. Some stones are available with one grit on either side. With or without a teacher, using a sharpening stone is a skill that takes practice and perseverance, but one well worth your time and effort.

The late Al Buck of Buck knives fame had good advice for people struggling to learn to sharpen knives. He would start by telling people there were only three things to remember: "Always cut into the stone, never drag your knife edge back over the stone, and always maintain your angle." And he had this great tip: Take a marker and shade in the bevel of the knife. Take two strokes on the stone and then examine the edge of the blade. If you have maintained the proper angle, all the black will be gone. If you see marker on the top edge, it means you are holding the back of the knife too far from the stone. If there is marker on the bottom edge but the top is clean, you are letting the knife lie too flat on the stone and you need to raise it a bit. Mark it again and keep practicing.

A final word on knives: no matter how careful you are, there's a very high likelihood that at some point, you're going to bleed. Our recommendation: If it's a minor cut (as is most likely), take a quick break to wash the cut with hot soapy water, slap on a bandage (or if you're outside, apply some chewed up yarrow leaves and flowers), and remember that your first knife cut is almost a rite of passage. If it's a more serious cut, seek help from a friend or parent while holding the cut hand over your head and applying pressure to the wound with your other hand. But whether your first cut is minor or less-than-minor, please don't let it stop you from mastering this essential tool.

PART ONE

HOW TO OUTRUN A BEAR

THE FIRST THING TO KNOW about how to outrun a bear is that you can't. That's because bears can run at speeds up to 40 miles per hour (that's 50 feet in 3 seconds!), while you, dear reader, are stuck in the low 20s. You don't have to be very good at math to figure that one out.

The second thing to know is that it's really, really unlikely you'll ever find yourself in a sketchy bear situation. Fact is, most bears don't want a thing to do with us humans, and unless you're threatening their young'uns or have just bathed in meat juice, they'll steer clear. Most often, you've surprised them as much as they've surprised you. If you are in an area where you might have an encounter (like a berry patch), make sure you are paying attention to your surroundings. This is not a good time to be wearing your ear buds. Singing, talking, or otherwise making your presence known will generally cause bears to head for the hills.

But none of this does you a whit of good if you do find yourself crossing paths with an ornery ursine. In this unlikely scenario, here's what to do:

1. Know your bears. This will help you assess the actual risk. Black bears (they're, um, black, and usually fairly small) are generally nonaggressive and don't view you as a meal. That said, if they are demonstrating aggression, don't take any chances. Grizzly bears (brown, and not very small at all) have been known to dine on human meat, so you really don't want to mess around with them.

2. Every piece of your body and mind is going to be screaming at you to freak out, but it's important to remain calm. Yell "get out of here, you big ole bear!" or "I'm not tasty, I'm not tasty!" while raising your arms and waving them around so you look even bigger than you are.

3. As you're yelling, back away real slow and steady. Oh, and don't make eye contact; the bear might view that as a sign of aggression.

4. Some people will tell you that if the bear is still advancing, you should climb a tree. We would like to dispel this popular myth once and forever. *Do not* climb a tree, unless you favor the idea of being clawed mercilessly out of it. Black bears are excellent climbers, and grizzlies have been known to attack people who climb trees to escape. So yeah: no trees.

5. *If* the bear charges, you still have a good chance. That's because bears are known to bluff charge, giving their enemy one last chance to back down. Stand your ground, make yourself as big as you can, and yell loudly "I told you to get the heck outta here!" or something to that effect.

6. As a last resort, use your pepper spray (you do have pepper spray, right?). Start spraying when the bear is 10 to 20 yards away. Aim for the eyes, and prepare for the bear to be disoriented, giving you the perfect opportunity to slip away.

7. Here's where we get to dispel another myth: If you are attacked, it's not always best to play dead. Indeed, if it's a black bear and you can't escape to a safe place, fight with all you've got, concentrating blows to the face. Because they're smaller and more timid than grizzlies, you have an excellent chance of fending them off. But if it's a grizzly, the popular advice is correct: lie flat on your stomach with your hands clasped behind your neck. Spread your legs to make it harder for the bear to turn you over. Remain still until the bear has left the area. Chances are, they'll lose interest, but if the attack persists, fight back using whatever you have on hand to hit the bear in the face.

FORECAST THE WEATHER

BACK WHEN PIRATES ROAMED the seven seas, there was no such thing as a weather app or Weather.com or even a local TV meteorologist. Those grizzled old plundering sailors needed to know the weather as much as anyone alive today, but they had nothing but their senses and experience to rely on. Here's how they did it.

LOOK TO THE SKY

The clouds are your first indicator of upcoming weather. We've all seen those low, dark, mean-looking clouds that blow in right before a thunderstorm, and we're all familiar with those puffy-white-dancing-sheep sort of high clouds that come with good weather. But with just a little practice, it's possible to know much further ahead of time what the weather's likely to bring.

CUMULONIMBUS

MAMMATUS

CIRRUS

ALTOCUMULUS

CUMULUS TOWERS

NIMBOSTRATUS

➤ **Cumulonimbus clouds** are dense and tall, formed by water vapor carried on upward air currents. They look like huge stacks of mashed potatoes. The development of cumulonimbus clouds generally means there's a good chance of severe weather in the near future.

➤ **Mammatus clouds** are formed by sinking air, and they can bring thunderstorms of varying intensity. They look a bit like upside-down cumulonimbus clouds or udders on cows.

➤ **Cirrus clouds,** also known as "mare's tails," are found high in the sky, like long streamers or . . . you guessed it, tails. If you see these, be ready for bad weather within the next 36 hours or so.

➤ **Altocumulus clouds** also suggest poor weather in the next 36 hours; they're a little harder to define, but they look like lots of small, loosely connected globs. Some people say they look like fish scales, hence the term "mackerel skies."

➤ **Cumulus towers,** which are stacks of those perfect, puffy clouds that appear on mostly sunny days, indicate the possibility of showers later in the day—but generally only if they appear as towers.

➤ **Nimbostratus clouds** are low and heavy and cover lots of the sky, sort of like frosting on cake; they mean rain is imminent, unless you're getting wet even as you're looking at them, in which case they mean it's raining *now.*

➤ **Cloud cover** on a winter night means you should expect warmer weather, because clouds prevent the heat radiation that lowers the temperature on clear nights.

OTHER TRICKS

You might have heard the old saying "Red sky at night, sailor's delight; red sky in morning, sailors take warning." Like their pirate cousins, those old sailors knew a thing or two about a thing or two. So if you see a red sky during sunset, it means there's a high-pressure system with dry air that's stirring dust particles in the air (that's what makes the red color). Since weather usually moves from west to east, this means the dry air is heading in your direction.

A red sky in the morning, however, means that the dry air has already moved past you, and what follows is at least somewhat likely to be a low-pressure system carrying moisture.

Here's another proverb for you: "Circle around the moon, rain or snow soon." This is because the ring around the moon is caused by light shining through cirrostratus clouds associated with warm fronts and moisture. Expect precipitation within the next three days.

Check the direction of the wind by throwing a few stems of grass into the air. Easterly winds (blowing from the east) can indicate an approaching storm front, while westerly winds predict good weather. Strong winds happen during pressure differences, which is often a sign of advancing storm fronts.

Check the grass for dew at sunrise. The dewier the grass, the lesser the chance of rain that day. Dry grass indicates overnight clouds or strong breezes, both of which are signs of approaching rain.

Smell the air. Take a deep, slow breath through your nose. Plants release their waste in a low-pressure atmosphere, resulting in a composty sort of smell that suggests upcoming rain. And in general, scents are stronger in moist air; even the flowers smell better just before it rains.

Watch the birds. If they're flyin' high, it means a decent chance of fair weather. That's because the falling air pressure associated with storms causes discomfort in birds' ears, causing them to stay closer to the ground.

Listen to the frogs. More frogs call, and calls get louder, if rain is on the way. When frogs mate they lay their eggs in bodies of fresh water. More rain means more places to lay eggs, so the males increase their efforts to attract females.

Of course, even with all these tricks up your sleeve, it's essential to be prepared for surprises, so don't leave your rain gear or extra layers at home when you go wandering.

TAP A MAPLE TREE

IF YOU LIVE IN THE NORTHEAST, upper Midwest, or mid-Atlantic you probably have maple trees somewhere nearby. Which is good, because not only are maples really pretty, their sap is remarkable stuff.

Early settlers in the northeastern United States and Canada learned about maple trees from Native Americans. Various legends explain the initial discovery; a University of Vermont blog about the history of maple (https://blogs.lt.vt.edu/amstfood/maple-syrup) shares a story that goes like this:

The Creator had at first made life too easy for his People by filling the maple trees with a thick syrup that flowed year-round. One day, Glooskap, a mischievous young man, found a village of his People strangely silent—the cooking fires were dead, weeds had overtaken the gardens. Glooskap discovered the villagers laying in the woods, eyes closed, letting the syrup from the maple trees drip into their mouths. Glooskap brought fresh water from the lake and using his special power filled the trees with water

MAPLE

until the syrup ran from them thin and fast. He then ordered his people up, telling them that the trees were no longer filled with the maple syrup, but only a watery sap. He told them they would have to hunt and fish and tend their gardens for sustenance. He promised that the sap would run again, but only during the winter when game is scarce, the lake is frozen, and crops do not grow.

Legends aside, no one knows for sure how humans figured out that maple sap could be boiled down to make syrup and sugar, but they did, and maple sweetener soon became an important source of energy and nutrition. That's because maple sap is loaded with minerals and antioxidants that aren't found in white sugar and corn syrup.

To harvest maple sap, the indigenous people of North America made a slash in a sugar maple with a stone ax and inserted a wooden wedge to direct the sap into birch bark containers like the one you can make on page 134. Then they boiled the sap, first in wooden troughs and later in iron or copper kettles.

Now, you can't just saunter out your door and do this any ole time of year; that's because sap runs on days with the temperature is above freezing following a night when it's dropped below freezing. Depending on your location, this is going to be late winter to early spring.

One more thing to know before you get started: Maple sap looks like water because it mostly *is* water—98 percent water, in fact. This means it's going to take about 40 gallons of sap to make 1 gallon of syrup. A healthy, productive sugar maple tree should produce enough sap in one season to make about a quart of syrup, though there are many variables.

TRY IT YOURSELF, (ROUGHLY) THE TRADITIONAL WAY

1. Make a few spiles (that is, spigots, or taps) out of branches with soft, porous, "pithy" centers that are easy to hollow out. Sumac is a good one. Cut 6- to 8-inch sections and use a knife to split them in half longways. Scrape out the pith and carve one end narrow enough to fit in a $7/16$-inch hole.

2. Make a few birch bark containers (see page 134), or use any kind of watertight container, such as used milk jugs. Not to state the obvious, but the taller the sides, the more sap they hold.

3. Find a few sugar maples.

4. Don't slash the trees with an ax! It is way too hard on the tree. Instead, drill holes about $7/16$ inch in diameter about 3 feet off the ground at a slight upward angle into each tree. One tap per tree is best for the longevity of the tree.

5. Use a hammer (or a poor man's hammer, aka a rock) to gently tap the spiles into the holes.

6. Position the containers at the bases of the trees so they will catch the sap.

7. Now wait for a warm, sunny day after a night when the temperature dropped below freezing, and check to see if the sap is running out of the spiles. If it is, take a good long swig of the stuff. This slightly sweet drink has traditionally been appreciated as a spring tonic, full of minerals and enzymes to cleanse and recharge the body for the busy summer season. You can also use maple sap to make tea or to replace water in cooking. It takes at least a gallon of sap to make about half a cup of maple syrup, so unless you can collect a few gallons, just enjoy the sap as is.

8. If you have more than a few gallons, collect what you've got and put it in a pot on the stove or over a fire. As it boils, you'll notice it slowly become darker and thicker. It's truly maple syrup when it reaches 219 degrees and has a sugar content of 66.9 percent, but you don't have to be so exact. Just boil until it's dark and sweet and you can barely keep yourself from drinking every last drop.

TRY IT YOURSELF,
THE MORE MODERN WAY

1. Get a few maple taps (it isn't hard to find places online that sell them singly).

2. Find some plastic buckets, metal cans, milk jugs, or other containers. Metal sap buckets with lids and handy holes to hang on the taps are convenient but frequently sold only by the dozen, unless you live near a sugaring supplier. They're also sorta pricey.

3. Follow steps 3 to 8 on pages 13 and 14, and then pour yourself a hard-earned taste of the good stuff. Bottoms up!

FIND A WILD SNACK

THE THING ABOUT BEING IN THE WILD is that it's, um, wild. Therefore, it's really unlikely you're going to stumble across any fast food around the next beech tree. So it's handy to have a few tricks up your sleeve for those times when your belly's crying and the trail mix is long gone.

If you think this means you'll be reduced to licking moss off stream-side rocks, think again. That's because almost every species of plant that humans cultivate for food has one or more wild relatives; the most obvious examples are berries. Not exactly bad eatin'. See the sidebar about harvesting wild plants, "The Safe and Honorable Harvest," on page xiii before you get started. Wild berries are tasty, and you shouldn't pass them by. However, the woods are full of other snack foods that might be less obvious but will still put a smile on your face and fill your belly.

CATTAILS

Cattails are awesome in so many ways! The leaves can be made into baskets or visors (see page 130); the seed head can be used

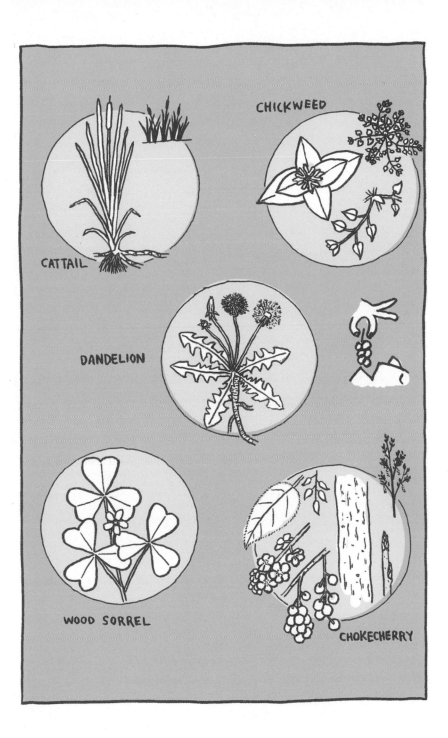

as tinder or dipped in fat and used as a torch; the fluff can be used as insulation in clothing, pillows, mattresses, and even life jackets. *And* it has edible parts at all different times of the year!

IDENTIFY IT

Cattails are found throughout North America and much of the rest of the Western Hemisphere. In fact, there is hardly a fresh or brackish body of water, marsh, or wetland that doesn't host these tall, slender-leafed plants with a "hot dog on a stick" seed head. Take a quick look at a book or internet photo and you're sure to recognize them.

EAT IT

Cattails serve as a food source for many Native American tribes, and it's easy to see why. Most of the plant is edible, from the roots (wash off the muck and boil 'em, or eat them raw), to the leaves (cook them like you would spinach), to the distinctive female flower spike that looks like a corndog (harvest in early summer, boil, and eat like corn on the cob). But the best part of cattails is the bottom of the stem, where it's mostly white. Boil this part of the plant or eat it raw: it tastes just like chicken. Actually, it doesn't taste like chicken at all, but it's still pretty darn good.

The other cool thing about cattails is that you can use the pollen as flour for cookies, muffins, pancakes, and the like. This only works in the spring, when the plants are blooming and the green spikes turn bright yellow with pollen. Place a plastic bag over the end of the plant and shake to capture the pollen. Use it as part of the flour in all your favorite recipes.

CHICKWEED

We used to consider chickweed an annoying and difficult-to-remove weed in the garden. But a lot of the reasons it drove us nuts in the garden are the things that make it a good wild edible: it grows in great abundance in the early spring when little else is growing, and it comes back quickly once harvested. Plus, it has a fresh sweetness that is a nice addition to salads and sandwiches.

IDENTIFY IT

Chickweed's Latin name is *Stellaria media*—*stellaria* means "little star," a reference to its white, star-shaped flowers. The leaves are smooth and oval shaped, and the delicate leaf stalk has a single line of hairs running up the stem. Among some reasonably close look-alikes, three things separate chickweed from poisonous pretenders. First, it does *not* have milky sap. Next, it has one line of hairs on its stem that changes sides with each pair of leaves. Last, if you bend the stem, rotate each end counter to each other, and pull gently, the outer part of the stem will separate but the elastic inner part will not, and you will have stretched the inner part between the two stem ends. Try it; it's pretty cool.

EAT IT

Chickweed has a delicious, fresh taste and is high in vitamins and minerals. It can be collected in early spring and again during the fall and into winter, depending on where you live.

The best way to eat chickweed is to add it to salads, put it on a sandwich, or just eat it by the handful while you're working outside. If you've got a sore throat, you can steep chickweed in boiling water for 10 minutes to make a tea. Drink a cup or three and you'll feel a whole bunch better.

DANDELION

Modern gardeners and lawn tenders think of this plant as an obnoxious weed, but our forefathers and -mothers treasured it so highly for its medicinal and culinary uses that they carried the seeds on the *Mayflower* to plant when they arrived in the New World. Now that's love—yet another example of a common-knowledge treasure that has been lost in the march of "progress."

IDENTIFY IT

Dandelions are found in virtually every kind of habitat, so you shouldn't have to look too hard to find them. You probably know a dandelion when you see it, if its distinctive yellow flower is on display—but when the flowers are not blooming it's easy to be confused by the many look-alikes that have similar leaves. Remember that dandelion leaves are hairless, have deep notches, and grow around the stem in a rosette. The leaves and hollow stems grow directly from the rootstock. Dandelions have only one flower per stem, in contrast to look-alike plants that have branching stems. The root, leaves, and stems of a dandelion all exude a milky white sap, making this an exception to the rule of avoiding plants with milky sap.

EAT IT

Not only is every part of the dandelion plant edible—leaves, flowers, and roots—but it's also a nutritional powerhouse, with 50 percent more vitamin C than tomatoes, more iron and calcium than spinach, and more potassium than bananas.

The leaves are most tender in early spring, when they can be eaten raw in salads and out of hand. They can also be steamed, boiled, or sautéed. Our favorite things to do with dandelion leaves are to sauté them with lots of butter and garlic or add them to soups. As the leaves age and are exposed to sunlight they become more bitter. But soon the buds appear, and these can be used in the same ways as the leaves; the key to eating the buds is picking them early when they are still tight little buttons close to the base of the plant.

The buds open into yellow flowers that have a surprisingly sweet and mild flavor. The base of the flower head is bitter, especially the green sepals that look like small leaves. Pinch them off and ditch 'em. Pull the petals off and sprinkle them in salads or add them to scrambled eggs, pancakes, or muffins.

The roots of dandelions have excellent medicinal value and can also be used as a coffee substitute or to make a delicious tea. Dig the roots in the fall, wash them well, and hang them until they're completely dry. Then use clippers to cut them into small pieces. Put the pieces on a baking tray and roast them in the oven for about 30 minutes at 350 degrees; the pieces need to be brown and dried all the way through so they will grind and for long-term storage. If you're looking to use the roots for a coffee-like drink, at this point let the roasted pieces cool and then grind them in a coffee grinder. If you want more of a tea, you can just use the pieces.

Put 6 tablespoons of ground or cut-up dandelion root into a pint of boiling water and leave to steep for 30 minutes or longer (depending on taste). Strain this infusion into a saucepan and reheat. Drink as is—or even better, add milk and sweetener.

WOOD SORREL

Humans have used wood sorrel for food and medicine for millennia. The taste is mildly lemony, in a deliciously sour way. Wood sorrel is found all over the world, and every part of the plant is edible all year long, raw or cooked. Best of all, wood sorrel has no dangerous look-alikes, so you can stuff your face to your heart's content. It's even loaded with vitamin C and probably some other good things we don't know about.

IDENTIFY IT

Numerous species of wood sorrel grow throughout North America. All of them are small, delicate herbs with very thin stems. Their leaf shape is the clincher for recognizing them; each leaf consists of three symmetrical leaflets radiating from a single point like clover leaflets. Unlike clovers, however, each wood sorrel leaflet is distinctly heart-shaped. They are usually strongly creased along the mid-vein, like a folded paper heart. The flowers have five pedals and are yellow, pink, or white depending on species.

Once you've found it, you'll find it easy to identify in the future.

EAT IT

We like wood sorrel best as a nibbling, rabbity kind of snack. It often grows trailside or right in the semishady spot you've decided to lounge around in on a summer's day, almost like it was just waiting for you to come along. Young plants that haven't yet flowered are best, but all above ground parts are edible.

The greens are an excellent lemony addition to salads. Or use them to make some lemonade! Gather a pile of wood sorrel, chop the plants finely, steep them in cold water for a few hours, strain out the greens, and add a little sweetener. (We like maple syrup, but honey or sugar work as well.)

TEN THINGS TO DO WITH TREE PITCH

WE'VE ALL GOTTEN ACCUSTOMED to going to the store and buying some kind of commercial product to meet our every minor passing need. Truthfully, that's a big part of the reason the world is in the state it's in. But it doesn't have to be this way. There's a treasure trove of woodland resources that are (a) entirely free and (b) perpetually regenerating. We don't know about them because this wisdom has been lost across the generations and they are not always obvious to the untrained eye.

Case in point: the resin, commonly known as "pitch," that trees (particularly conifers) secrete to close wounds is an amazingly handy substance that you might call "nature's duct tape." Pitch serves as a sealant over the tree's injury, hardening into an amber-colored glob that darkens over time. The fresher the glob, the more sticky and pliable it is, and sticky and pliable is what you're going to want when you go to use it. For harvesting, it's preferable to use an old knife or even a sturdy stick, so you don't get your good knife blade sticky. That said, if all you've got on hand is your favorite blade, go ahead and use it: We tell you how to clean it in the sidebar on page 27.

To find pitch, you have a couple of options. You could grab a tree ID book and head for the woods to track down some good pitch trees, like pine, spruce, fir, cedar, and tamarack. Or you could just wander around the forest until you bump into a sticky, globby thing on a tree. Either way, when you find it, pry or scrape off your newfound prize. For some applications, you might need to heat the pitch or even give it some vigorous chewing to get it soft enough to use. Use for what, you say? So glad you asked.

HEAL YOURSELF

One of the amazing things about tree resin is that it's antiseptic, astringent, anti-inflammatory and antibacterial. Here are some ways to take advantage of those qualities:

 Apply a layer of pitch to a cleaned-out cut.

 Apply a soft glob to stop bleeding.

 Use it to treat skin rashes and eczema.

 Chew it straight off the tree for sore throats and colds.

MAKE GLUE

Pretty much anything you need to glue or patch in the woods can be fixed with tree pitch. For instance, try these uses:

Waterproof boot seams, canoes, and containers.

Patch holes in tents and tarps.

Glue feathers on an arrow.

CREATE FIRE, ILLUMINATION, OR HEAT

Pitch is highly flammable and impervious to water, so it's great for generating a reliable blaze that can provide you with warmth or light:

▶ To make an effective fire starter, especially in wet weather, add pitch to other natural tinder. (Split pine sticks that have streaks of resin in them are also good for this purpose.)

▶ To make a torch, melt some pitch, pour it on a cloth, wrap it around a green (that is, freshly cut) stick, and set it alight.

▶ To create a lamp, find a stone with a depression, a large shell, or a cupped piece of bark. Twist a piece of fabric or some dried moss to serve as a wick. Fill the depression with pitch and lay the wick material on top. Ignite the wick first, which will in turn ignite the resin. The resin will burn like a candle, and you can keep feeding it to maintain the flame. To use the lamp as a heat source, place a metal container that has plenty of air holes in it over the ignited pitch. The metal container will absorb the heat and conduct it to the surrounding area.

HOW DO I GET THIS &%$#@!! STICKY STUFF OFF MY KNIFE AND HANDS (AND NECK AND EYEBROWS)???

Don't swear: De-sticking pitch is actually super easy. If you are in the woods, rub dirt into the pitch so it isn't sticky and driving you bonkers anymore. When you get home, just rub any kind of oil or fat (vegetable oil, olive oil, lard) into your hands (and knife and neck and eyebrows). This pulls out the sap, at which point it all washes off with warm water and soap. No biggie.

USING BIRD LANGUAGE TO TRACK IN REAL TIME

CHECK THIS OUT: you are alive today because your ancestors were aware of what birds were talking about. That's because a lot of what birds talk about is potential predators, such as the big cats (and when we say "big cat," we're not talking about your everyday overfed house feline) that once roamed the plains and forests. For your ancestors, birds were nature's alarm system, alerting them to danger or assisting them in hunting their own food. You can learn to decipher bird language, too.

Birds send messages with both vocalization and body language. Bird vocalizations are not random or nonsensical. Every bird has specific vocalizations that are broadcast for very specific reasons. If we focus on a chickadee, we can see that its "heyy-sweeetie" song, which we often hear in the early part of the day, is an advertisement for a mate as well as a display of its territory and location as a male. Compare that to the sharper and harsher "chicka-dee-dee-dee" they use to scold your cat. The Carolina wren's alarm, "tsshk tssshk," has that same harsh tone and incites a feeling of urgency, even in us humans. These patterns show up wherever you live, whether California or Ghana. In fact, it's no coincidence parents "shhh-shhh" children to quiet them. We speak this language, having shared thousands of years of common predators with the birds.

A good foundation activity for learning bird language is having a sit spot, a specific place where you can return regularly to observe and feel what changes and what stays the same over time. Pick a single species at your sit spot: maybe juncos, robins, towhees, or sparrows. Figure out who the individual birds are that come to your spot. What are they concerned with on a daily basis? What are their most and least active times of day?

Bird language is a form of tracking, and, like ground tracking, we are always right if we track alone, which is why it's good to track with other people.

1. With a partner, find a place that has substantial bird activity. Morning to midday is a good time frame, since many birds take a siesta during the midafternoon hours. Look for birds that are dark or brown in color; these are good teachers because they evolved to live close to the earth, and thus they share things in common with you, such as awareness of approaching tigers and bears. Or even just deer. Meanwhile, bright yellow goldfinches are more concerned with hawks than ground predators.

2. Partner one sits while partner two moves around. Partner two should mix up their movements from sneaky to casual to creeping. Keep mixing up the body language; the point is to test the ways your body language impacts the behavior of the birds around you.

3. Leave the sight of partner one and come back after a short walk. Do all of this while partner one takes notes. How were the birds responding to partner two, if at all? Could you tell when partner two was returning before you saw them? Were mammals such as squirrels or chipmunks responding to partner two? What was partner two's experience while moving around? How did they feel the birds responded to their movement?

4. Another variation on this activity is to have one of the partners sneak off and hide somewhere on the land. The other partner will wait about 2 minutes and then try to find the hidden partner. If the hidden partner wants to, they can try moving around as they, too, listen for the potential alarms caused by the searcher. It is important to have some agreed-upon time or signal, like a loud whistle or a holler, to determine the end of the game.

5. Trackers can also actively practice and study ways to be invisible in the forest and ways to avoid creating splashes of alarm that ripple out through the wild critters. That deer quietly walking away before we see it is informed by the robin that we startled as we walked briskly into the woods. Being invisible means respecting the birds and mammals in our environment and acknowledging them as we move around. When we see a ground bird such as a robin, there is a moment that we can offer some respect and space for that robin to carry on with its daily routine. Often people don't notice that first moment when the robin notices us, but instead they push right through its comfort zone and cause an agitation alarm. To avoid causing this sort of alarm, try to direct your body slightly away from the bird or mammal. Turn a quarter turn and avoid eye contact. Let your body be relaxed and not held tensely like a predator. You can even stop to eat an occasional wild edible plant to exhibit that your intention is not hunting.

EAT A BUG!

HERE'S SOMETHING you may not want to know about eating insects, but we're going to tell you, anyway: you already are. That's because food manufacturers are legally allowed a certain number of "defects" in their products, which includes insects. For instance, an 8-ounce handful of raisins might contain up to 35 fruit fly eggs, and 240 "pests" are allowed in each 12-ounce bag of frozen broccoli (what we want to know is: who's doing the counting?). "OK, fine," you say. "I never liked raisins and broccoli all that much anyhow. I'll just eat chocolate instead." In which case, you should know that a chocolate bar is allowed eight insect parts. And no, you don't get to choose which ones.

Truth is, this isn't really such a bad thing, because insects are loaded with the vital macronutrients of protein and fat. And tasty? Whoo-eee, yes. You haven't lived until you've tried grasshoppers fried in soy sauce. Did you know that 80 percent of the world's population eats over one thousand species of insects? Well, now you do.

While the majority of bugs are perfectly safe to eat, there are a few precautions you should take if you decide to eat insects yourself. Don't eat any insects that are brightly colored; in general, such coloration is a warning to predators that they're toxic. Avoid hairy

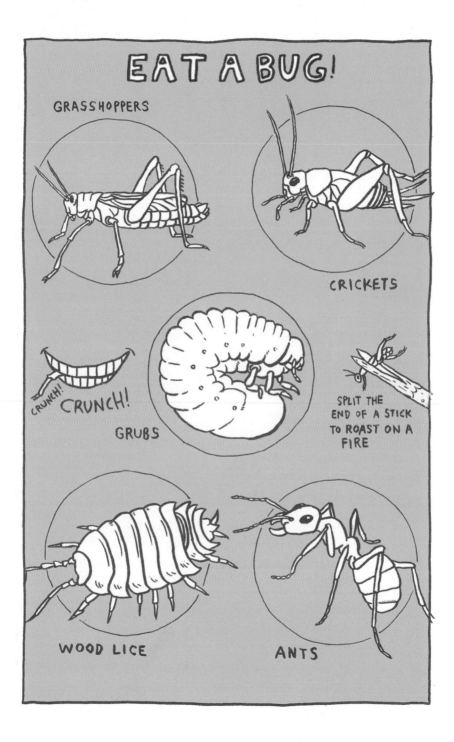

bugs; there may be stingers nestled in the fuzz. Also avoid any bugs that have a potent smell (except, paradoxically, stinkbugs).

Whenever possible, you should cook your insects before you eat them, since they may carry parasites or harmful bacteria that won't survive cooking (this is true of all meat, by the way, so don't think there's anything particularly gross about insects). Besides, cooking improves flavor and makes the nutrients more digestible.

There are loads of edible insects out there, but we are only going to speak to the ones we have actual experience ingesting *and* didn't find utterly disgusting (like the earthworm our son chewed up and swallowed when he was eight and had just read *How to Eat Fried Worms*).

These five tasty tidbits are easy to find, nutritious, and have tastes that could plausibly be acquired. We encourage you to give them a try—or at the very least choke them down when you're really hungry. And if that's not convincing enough, just imagine the look on your friends' faces when you casually pop a grub in your mouth and start chewing.

➤ GRASSHOPPERS are extraordinarily protein-rich, and you can collect them pretty much anywhere.

> **Catch 'em**: Grasshoppers are easiest to catch by hand in the early morning when they move more slowly. Sweeping a butterfly net across the tops of tall grass is pretty effective.

> **Eat 'em**: Remove the wings and legs, skewer them, and roast over a flame. Dry roast them with a splash of soy sauce at the end, fry them up in garlic butter, or make them into fritters. The possibilities are endless.

CRICKETS are super nutritious and taste pretty darn good.

Catch 'em: Crickets can be caught by hand, but they are fast. You can get them to come to you by burying a plastic container in the ground and baiting it with a piece of ripe fruit. Leave it overnight, and in the morning your breakfast will be hopping. Look for crickets in damp, dark places: under rocks and logs are good bets. Also look in tall grass, in shrubs, and in trees.

Eat 'em: Crickets have a subtle, nutty flavor, almost like popcorn. Roast them, then salt them or season them with spices (or both), and eat them whole as a snack. Other options? Chocolate-coat them, or throw a handful into rice.

GRUBS Don't act surprised, you knew it was coming! Hey, grubs (which are really just the larvae of insects) are easy to find and they don't exactly scurry along.

Catch 'em: The best place to find grubs is in rotting logs. Use a stick or a rock to break the wood apart and sift through to find your morsels. You can also try searching under rocks and leaf litter.

Eat 'em: Grubs can be eaten raw, but as with all of these little treats, it's better to cook them first. Skewer them lengthwise with a stick and cook over an open flame until the skin is crispy.

WOOD LICE (also known as pill or potato bugs). This critter is actually a terrestrial crustacean, not an insect, which is maybe why they seem to taste a bit like shrimp.

Catch 'em: These guys don't move too fast, either, so it's easy to collect an abundance. Turn over rocks and logs and sift through dead leaves: you're sure to come across some.

Eat 'em: Boil them in water. They can carry nematodes, so be sure they're thoroughly cooked. When they're done, chow down.

➤ **ANTS** are everywhere, easy to catch, and actually taste good.

Catch 'em: Scan the ground for a few minutes and you are likely to find one. They hang out in groups (called an "army"), so where you find one there are sure to be more. Many, many more. Finding an anthill is an efficient way to get a whole bunch. If you put a stick in the hole it will soon be covered in ants and you can shake them off into a container. Put them into a container of water while you're collecting so they don't get away. A few hundred make a nice snack.

Eat 'em: Again, you can eat them raw, but it's better not to. If you do, make sure they're dead or they might bite you while you are trying to bite them. Put them on a baking tray, salt them, and roast them in the oven at 225 degrees until dry and crispy. Different ant species have slightly different flavors, but most have varying degrees of ascorbic acid in them, lending them a slightly lemony flavor (an ant-like lemony flavor, that is).

SEE ANIMALS BEFORE THEY SEE YOU

CRAZY AS IT SOUNDS NOW, when pretty much everybody walking down the street is twitching their thumbs on a smartphone, it wasn't so long ago that humans relied on their keen sense of awareness to keep them alive. Staying focused and tuned into the world around us was essential to finding dinner or to avoid becoming dinner.

Cultivating mindful awareness in the natural world or anywhere else we wander has other benefits for humans today: maintaining that direct connection to our surroundings is the key to actually giving a fig about our surroundings. If we don't notice and observe, we don't tend to care, and when we don't care we tend to stay silent even as species go extinct, or the planet warms, or the flotillas of plastic in the oceans grow with every bag we discard. The same benefit goes for our relationship to other humans; when we engage face-to-face, with genuine interest in one another, we have a much harder time being mean and discriminatory and judgmental. All of which is to say that if you develop the sensory awareness you need to observe wildlife, that same awareness will increase your curiosity, compassion, and appreciation of *everything*.

On top of all this good stuff, cultivating a sense of awareness will empower you to notice things that have been right under your nose all along—you just didn't know it. If you spend any time at all in the woods, you have been seen, heard, and definitely smelled by more wild animals than you can imagine. Now it is your turn to sense them first.

WALK LIKE A FOX

"Fox walking" is a technique for walking silently through the woods, so named because a stalking fox takes slow, deliberate, and silent steps with precise foot placement.

1. The first thing you need to do is liberate your paws (aka "feet") from your shoes. Socks off, too!

2. Now, it's all about how your feet connect with the ground; practice walking so that the first part of your body to contact the earth is the outside ball of your foot, right below your littlest toe.

3. Now roll your foot sideways until the inside ball is also in contact with the ground.

4. Lastly, lower your heel so that your entire foot is in engaged with the forest floor. Another advantage of this technique is that you're less likely to come down hard on sharp objects.

5. As you move forward, place your feet directly in front of one another; this creates the least disturbance possible and encourages thoughtful foot placement.

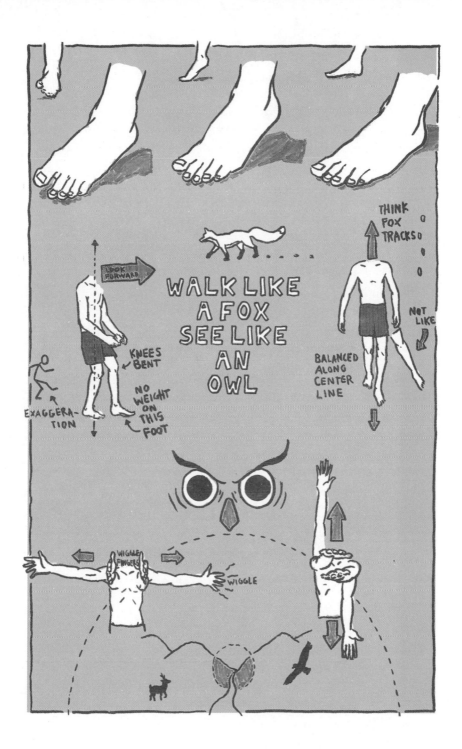

SEE LIKE AN OWL

Owls don't actually have eye*balls*; instead, their eyes are long and shaped like a tube. This shape makes them unable to move their eyes in the socket (which means they can't roll their eyes at their parents, unfortunately), but they are adept at looking straight ahead while taking in everything around them. Of course, they can turn their necks just about all the way around, which helps just a bit.

Our predecessors needed owl-like levels of awareness, relying on their entire peripheral vision—basically the opposite of what we do today when we focus narrowly on little screens, tunneling our vision to only what is directly in front of us.

1. To cultivate "owl eyes," spread your arms out as wide as you can and look straight ahead.

2. Keeping your head straight, wiggle your fingers and adjust your vision so you can see the digits of both hands moving at the same time.

3. Now notice that even when you are looking straight ahead, you can see a piece of the ground below you and even of the sky above. With this new level of awareness, you will be more likely to catch the twitch of a deer's ear or the tail wag of a squirrel out of the corner of your eye.

HEAR LIKE A DEER

Deer ears are like small satellite dishes. They tip back and forth, swivel, and turn to catch the slightest sounds. Our ears may be lacking in size and swivelability (that's a highly technical term; use at your own risk), but we can still expand their powers.

1. Cup your hands around your ears. Experiment with cupping just one ear, then the other, then both. Experiment with your hands in front of your ears, palms back (to hear behind you), and with your hands behind your ears, palms forward (to hear in front of you).

2. Try to figure out what sounds are coming from which direction.

3. Close your eyes and notice if it enhances your hearing (hint: it will).

4. See if you can pick out separate sounds, like individual bird songs.

In addition to these exercises, continue to expand your awareness by slowing your breath down. Breathe gently but deeply. Try to differentiate between individual odors.

"STOP" TO SURVIVE A NIGHT IN THE WOODS

IT IS SURPRISINGLY EASY to get turned around and twisted up in the woods and think you are heading right back to your campsite—only to find yourself caught between a thousand-foot cliff and a raging river, with a pack of snarling wolves closing in fast.

Acronyms as memory devices can seem a little absurd, but if you've just passed the tree with bleached human bones at its base for the fourth time and it sinks in that you're lost, this might be a good moment to STOP.

Sit down and stay put until the fear, frustration, and even panic has left your system. (Unless there really are wolves . . . in which case, run.)

THINK

Once you're calmed down and clear, review your situation calmly. What do you have that can help you? If you follow the advice elsewhere in this book (see page 63), you should have plenty. But at the very least, you'll have your common sense. And the truth you probably won't hear from the manufacturers trying to sell gadgets is this: your mind is your greatest survival tool.

OBSERVE

Check out your surroundings carefully. Did you tell people where you were going? If so, they might be searching for you. Even if you didn't tell anyone, look for an open area where searchers will have a better chance of seeing you. Look for natural shelter, or materials you can use to create shelter. Water's pretty darn important, too.

PLAN

In most cases, your list of priorities should look like this:

1. Find or make a shelter (see pages 100 and 122).

2. Build a fire for heat (see page 48).

3. Signal to attract attention. If you have a cellphone, use it! Build a smoky fire. Whistle loudly (see page 161).

4. Find water.

If after several days of waiting no one comes to your rescue (darn them, anyway!), you might have to face the possibility that no one is looking for you or that they're looking in all the wrong spots. In this case, you may decide to find your own way to safety (see page 45).

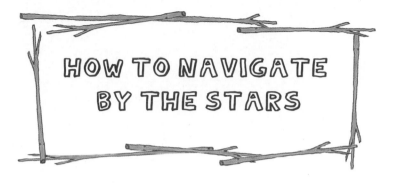

HOW TO NAVIGATE BY THE STARS

BELIEVE IT OR NOT, people used to find their way across thousands of miles before the GPS was invented and even before they had compasses. Folks tend to think that navigating by the stars is one of those things that can only be done if you wear an eye patch, carry a sword, or have a parrot on your shoulder. Fact is, celestial navigation can be learned in less time than it takes to learn how to read a compass, and it's just as accurate. Best part is, no eye patch, sword, or parrot necessary (which is not to say they wouldn't be pretty cool to have around).

The first step toward celestial navigation is locating and identifying Polaris, aka the North Star. That's because Polaris is the one star in the night sky that does not appear to move; it hangs out within a degree of the north celestial pole, and it is always in a northerly direction. One easy way to find Polaris is to first locate the famous star formation known as the Big Dipper (part of the constellation Ursus Major), which looks like a cup with a long handle. Since the Big Dipper rotates counterclockwise around Polaris, it will sometimes appear to be on its side, or upside down, or anywhere in between. But one thing that never changes is its relationship to the North Star.

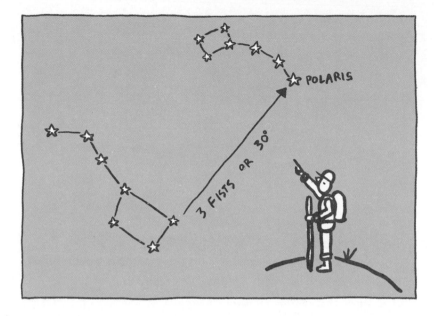

Next, locate the "pointer" stars in the Big Dipper's cup; these are the two stars that liquid would spill from if you were actually using the Dipper as a dipper. If you continue an imaginary line off these two stars for five times the distance between them, the line will end at the North Star (which is actually the brightest star in the constellation known as the Little Dipper).

Now that you've located your steadfast waypoint, all you need to do is face directly toward it. Hold your left arm straight to the left. That's west. Hold your right arm straight to the right. That's east. Your butt is facing south.

If you forget how to find Polaris, don't sweat it. You can actually find north using any old star:

▶ Drive two stakes in the ground 3 feet apart.

▶ Pick any star, but the brighter the easier.

▶ Line the star up with the tops of both stakes.

▶ The Earth's rotation from *west* to *east* causes the stars in the sky to rotate from *east* to *west.* If you wait for the star to move out of position and note which way it moved, it will tell you which direction you are facing:

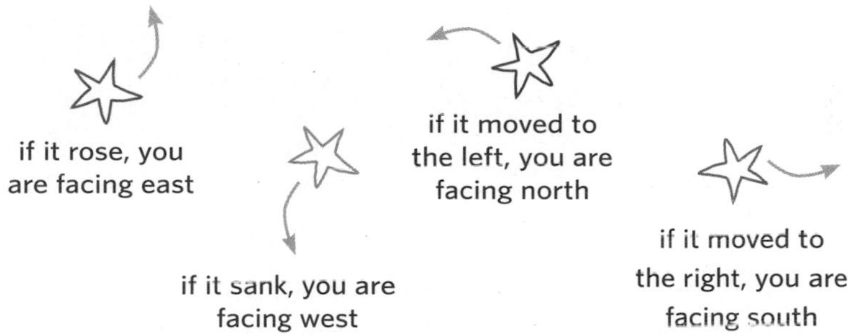

if it rose, you
are facing east

if it moved to
the left, you are
facing north

if it sank, you are
facing west

if it moved to
the right, you are
facing south

Yes, it's simple. And yes, it works.

MAKE A FRICTION FIRE

FOR TENS OF THOUSANDS OF YEARS, people have been making fire by rubbing sticks together. The action of rubbing things together creates friction, which causes heat. In the case of sticks, heat coaxes the wood into a smoldering coal. If you feed this coal with tinder and oxygen, it will become a fire. Which is real handy if you're freezing to death or sitting next to a big pile of raw meat. Or a package of marshmallows, for that matter.

Nothing is more empowering than knowing you have the means to create a crackling fire from nothing more than a couple of sticks and a piece of string. Two skills are involved in the craft of "friction fire": the first is making a bow-and-drill kit; the second is actually using the kit to start a fire.

MAKING A FIRESTARTER KIT

A bow-and-drill kit consists of a bow, a spindle (the drill), a fireboard, and a handhold.

MAKE FIRE FROM STICKS

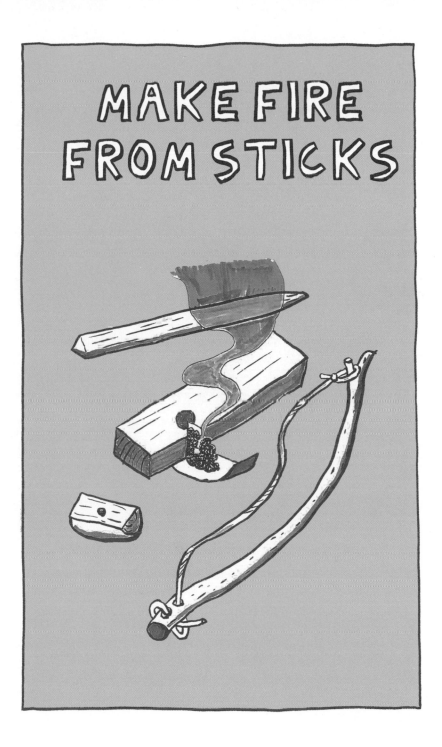

BOW

To make your bow drill you'll need a slightly curved branch about
2 feet long and about ¾ inch in diameter and some strong nylon
string (parachute cord or quarter-inch braided rope from a hardware store is a good choice). The kind of wood doesn't matter as
long as it is strong enough to not break. Cut a shallow notch an
inch in from each end of the bow, ¼ inch wide. Using a clove
hitch (see page 74), attach the string to each end of the bow with
enough slack in it so it can barely be wrapped around the spindle
once (see below) and be pretty tight.

SPINDLE

The spindle should be a dry branch or a split piece of dry wood
carved into a cylinder ½ inch to ¾ inch in diameter and 8 or so
inches long. The kind of wood will depend on where you live, but
in general, any soft nonresinous wood should work—try willow,
poplar, cottonwood, cedar, birch, ash, or basswood. Use a knife
to smooth your spindle into as perfect a cylinder as you can, cut
the top so it tapers to a point, and cut the bottom so it tapers to
a blunt point.

FIREBOARD

The fireboard should be made of the same type of wood as the
spindle, or at least the same hardness of wood. The drier the wood,
the better. It should be about half an inch thick, at least an inch
wide, about 8 inches to a foot long, and reasonably flat on both
sides. You can split this out from a log or whittle down a branch to
make a plank. The fireboard does not need to be a perfect rectangle
—mostly it just needs to sit flat and be relatively flat on top. On

one end, a spindle's width from the edge, make an indentation by putting your knife on the board and twisting—later you'll burn a hole into this spot for the spindle.

HANDHOLD

A handhold will let you apply pressure to the top of the spindle without hurting your hand. Find a piece of hardwood that fits comfortably in your palm. A chunk of hardwood branch split in half so the rounded side curves into your palm works real slick. Use your knife to make a depression in the flat side, in the same way you did in the fireboard. This hole needs some lubricant; there should be as little friction as possible on this end. It helps to make your handhold out of green (live) wood. You could also stuff a few green leaves or conifer needles in the hole.

Straight up, be aware that starting a friction fire is not a skill you'll master overnight. You'll get some heat, then you'll get some smoke, then your spindle will flip out of the string and you'll have to start over. Then you'll get some more smoke, then you'll start sweating and your arm will get tired, and you'll realize the notch in your fireboard isn't big enough. If you are sweating and swearing and getting exhausted, you are right on track, but it also might help to take a break and walk away for a minute. Drink some water, stretch, take a deep breath, and give it another go. When you finally blow that tinder bundle into flames, you're gonna feel like a rock star, we promise.

Ready? Here goes:

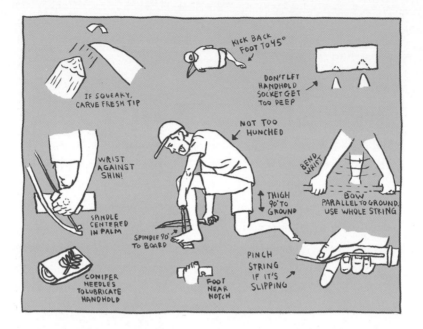

SET YOURSELF UP

Your posture will make all the difference as you work to start your friction fire. It can be helpful to have someone else observe to see if you're getting the right stance.

➤ Get down on one knee and hold the fireboard down with your left foot if you are right-handed and with your right foot if you are left-handed. The board should be directly under your arch. You will get a better grip barefooted. Put your foot as close as you can to the side of the depression you made with your knife.

➤ Put the knee that is on the ground directly behind the heel holding the fireboard. This might feel tippy at first, but that leg really needs to be out of the way of your bow moving back and forth. Kicking that back foot over toward the opposite side of your body at a 45-degree angle helps to stabilize things (see the illustration).

➤ To load the spindle, hold your bow in one hand and the spindle in the other, parallel to the string and next to it with the blunt end away from you. Tip the end of the spindle down and under the string, then twist it up and over the string so the string is wrapped once around the spindle on the side of the string away from the bow. If the spindle is between the bow and the string, it is wrong. It should be on the outside of the string and in the middle of the spindle (see the illustration). You will have to experiment with the tension on the string (we used a clove hitch so it can be easily undone and retied). The spindle should feel like it is about to pop out of the string if you don't hold it.

➤ Hold both the spindle and the bow with your dominant hand and put the end of the spindle in the depression in the fireboard. Pick up the handhold and put the depression in that on top of the spindle. Make sure the spindle is perpendicular to the fireboard. Put some downward pressure on the handhold and move your other hand back to the end of the bow.

➤ Keep the hand holding the handhold fairly straight and stiff and locked against your shin at the wrist (see the illustration). Use your body weight, not arm strength, to put the downward pressure on the handhold. The handhold should be perfectly flat and centered in your palm. If it's not, you will know it as you start to put on some pressure.

➤ Slowly and smoothly start to move the bow back and forth to spin the drill. Keep it parallel to the ground and use the whole length of string. Nice, long, smooth strokes are the key. Get used to the motion, and keep a steady rhythm.

➤ Start to move the bow faster and put more downward pressure on the handhold. You should see smoke coming from the bottom of the spindle. Keep going until you have burned a circle the width of the drill in the fireboard.

▶ Before going further, you need to cut a notch into the burned-out circle to let the dust fall onto your "coal catcher," a piece of bark or a sliver of wood that you'll place under the notch to catch the coal. Basically, you are cutting an eighth-inch pie slice out of the circle, starting from the center and going all the way to the edge of the board closest to you (see the illustration)—the more precise, the better. It helps to draw the notch on the board first, or etch a line with your knife. Then tip the board up on the opposite edge and use your knife to take small bites out of the wood on angles toward the center until the slice is cleaned out.

MAKE A TINDER BUNDLE

Tinder is dry, fluffy, fibrous material that catches fire easily. Once you have a coal, you'll put it into your tinder and blow it into a flame. Dry grasses, the inner bark of cedar trees, the fluff of a cattail seed head or the cattail's dry leaves, the seed head of phragmites (an invasive perennial grass), the inner bark of the basswood tree, and thin strips of birch bark (which works even when wet, due to the oils in birch) all make good tinder. Tinder should be rubbed together and buffed to break down the fibers. Do this over something to save the flammable powder that falls off.

Bundle your tinder into a ball with a depression in the center, like a bird's nest. Put the powder you saved into the center. It pays to take some time on this; there is nothing worse than finally getting that coal and not having good, ignitable tinder.

GOING FOR THE COAL

OK, now you're ready to make fire. All you need to add is a lot of patience and practice.

Put a coal catcher under the notch and set yourself up as you did for burning the hole in the fireboard, taking careful note of the positions of all your relevant body parts. Start the spindle drilling again, smoothly but quickly, applying as much downward pressure as you can, and going faster and faster. Get a good rhythm going and maintain it as long as you can. You should start to see smoke and then thicker, darker smoke and a little pile of black powder. *Don't stop!* Give it all you've got for ten more strokes. The time it takes to get an ember (glowing coal) depends on the wood you are using and how good your technique is. Experienced bow drillers make it look easy to get a coal in a few minutes. You will struggle at first, but with practice and persistence you will eventually get it, and it will be like someone flipped a switch.

I GOT A COAL, NOW WHAT?

If you stop and the smoke keeps coming, you probably have an ember. Don't gloat; you're not home free yet, because you still have to treat that ember gently and coax it into a fire. Tilt the fireboard away, protecting the ember from wind and your drops of sweat. If you put the ember into the tinder bundle too soon, it will die. Carefully waft air over it with your hand. It should start to solidify into a clump, continue smoking, and eventually glow red. Carefully use the coal catcher and transfer the ember to the nest of tinder, folding the bundle around it. Gently but firmly, blow on the bundle until it bursts into flames. The flames will be going upward, so don't worry immediately about burning your fingers. Most likely, the first time you succeed you will not be ready with kindling and firewood to start an actual fire, but no problem—now you can make fire any time you want! Just extinguish the tinder bundle in a safe manner; a container of water nearby is an easy precaution.

It's true that creating fire by friction takes a lot of practice, a good bit of sweat, and maybe even a four-letter word or two (such as "darn" and "argh"). But it's also true that it's one of the most useful, potentially life-saving skills in this book. And if that's not enough, it's definitely the most impressive one.

BE A WINTER EXPLORER!

DID YOU KNOW that in most modern cars, there are little dials you can turn, and that when you turn them, your butt gets hot? Of course you knew this, because we inhabit a culture and an era in which no one has to be the least bit uncomfortable, ever, no matter the weather. It seems like rain, snow, cold, heat, or any extreme weather—or any weather that's outside the boundaries of "perfect"—is an encroachment on the orderly existence of modern life. We have super-heated and -cooled homes, crazy insulated clothing for when we venture outside, and cars that won't even let our butts be cold for a minute. It's gotten to the point where a snowstorm isn't something to be enjoyed and to play in, but a hassle to be endured.

Forget all that, because there's really nothing better than exploring in winter. The forest is silent and still and beautiful, and the snow creates the world's biggest playground. You can slide over it, dig in it, pack it into balls and throw it (aka "a snowball fight"), or a million other things. And when you do get cold (and you will), there is simply nothing better than coming into a warm house for a cup of hot chocolate.

That said, winter fun isn't automatic; cold weather adventures definitely have the potential for wet, cold misery or just plain ole mediocrity. But like most things that take a little effort, being a winter explorer is worth it ten times over.

FIRST THINGS FIRST

Go with a buddy, tell someone at home where you're going, make sure you have a pack with the "ten essentials" (see page 64), and check the weather forecast! Fact is, these things are smart any time you head off to explore but never more so than in winter.

CLOTHING

Two words for dressing in cold weather: layers and wool. Wearing multiple layers will help you avoid sweating. Damp clothes next to your skin make you cold. Wool keeps you warm even when it gets wet. A second, generally less-expensive choice is synthetics, but whatever you do, stay the heck away from cotton. The phrase "cotton kills" is no joke, because nothing robs your body of heat like wet cotton.

Don't forget a hat and gloves. Extras in the pack are not a bad idea, especially gloves, as they get wet and lost easily.

FEET

If you're gonna have a good time out there, warm feet are essential, so make sure you wear insulated boots made for winter.

Heavier socks, or two pairs (or both), trap more warm air next to your skin and provide better insulation. Again, stick with wool. One caveat here is that too much sock thickness can mean a tight squeeze in your boots, which cuts off circulation. Make sure you can wiggle your toes.

Put your pants cuffs over the tops of your boots to keep the snow and wet out.

If you find your feet (or any other part of your body, for that matter) getting cold, *move*! Physical activity creates body heat and increases blood flow (and therefore heat) to your extremities.

FOOD AND DRINK

Your body burns more calories when it is trying to keep warm, so it stands to reason that you need more food and drink in winter. Always eat a good breakfast with plenty of protein and fat before going out, emphasizing stick-to-the-ribs stuff like cheese, meat, and nut butters.

Simple carbohydrates (think dried fruit and chocolate) metabolize almost immediately for a quick burst of energy and are good trail food, but it is best to eat them with a good amount of fat to avoid blood-sugar crashes.

On cold days, a hot drink is often all it takes to make life a whole lot better. A cup of tea or hot chocolate over a fire can make all the difference.

Don't forget that it is just as important to *stay hydrated* in winter as it is in summer. Drink plenty of water even if you don't feel particularly thirsty. If you are just a little bit dehydrated, your mental health and the way you function can become impaired, as well as your energy levels and resistance to cold.

OTHER THOUGHTS

We give up a lot by choosing to stay inside during what we've come to think of as "inclement" weather; it's worth pushing yourself a bit to experience all the good stuff so-called bad weather has to offer. If going outside for fun in winter is a stretch for you, find something you like to do to take your mind off the weather:

Ski, sled, or skate.

Look at the stars—they look clearer, sharper, and brighter this time of year.

Track animals—it's easier to see tracks in the snow.

Make a fire.

Hunt, trap, or ice fish—contact your local fish and wildlife department for information on how to get started.

Look for birds—they are easier to spot when the leaves have fallen.

Build a snow cave or a snowperson.

Have a snowball fight.

PART TWO

TEN ESSENTIALS
FOR THE
GREAT OUTDOORS

THE FUNNY THING ABOUT MISHAPS is that they generally don't happen when you *most* expect them; it's almost always when you *least* expect them. Admittedly, this is pretty inconvenient, but it's also just the way things are, so all we can do is prepare ourselves as best as possible.

That's why it's a really good idea to have a small backpack full of mishap-busting essentials, ready to hit the trail on even the shortest hikes (you know, the ones where you least expect anything to happen). The original "ten essentials" checklist was first assembled in the 1930s by the Mountaineers, a Seattle, Washington–based organization for climbers and outdoor adventurers, and it consisted of individual items such as a compass or matches. It has evolved to become a list of functional systems, like navigation or fire, but it has stood the test of time and is still just as relevant for outdoor adventurers today:

1. Navigation (map and compass)

2. Sun protection (sunglasses and sunscreen)

3. Insulation (extra clothing)

4. Illumination (headlamp, flashlight)

5. Medical care (first-aid supplies)

6. Fire (waterproof matches, lighter, candles)

7. Repair kit and tools (knife or multi-tool, duct tape)

8. Nutrition (extra food)

9. Hydration (extra water)

10. Emergency shelter (light tarp, space blanket, even a plastic trash bag)

One last thing to keep in mind: these items have no value unless you know how to use them. As one search and rescue leader said, "People talk about the ten essentials, but the most important essential is between your ears." We agree.

FIND THE BEST SPOT TO PITCH YOUR TENT

THERE'S NOTHING LIKE A POORLY SITED TENT to turn an otherwise completely awesome camping trip into something out of a bad movie. And there's nothing more relaxing than knowing you've got your tent pitched in the perfect spot, just waiting for the sun to go down, the campfire to burn to ashes, and the final s'more to be eaten. Here's how to pick the best tent site ever:

1. Unless you like the idea of waking up smeared against the wall of your tent with your campmates piled on top of you, snoring and drooling in your ear, find a flat spot. If you can't find perfectly flat ground, be sure to put your head on the high side; it's not ideal, but it's way more comfortable than the other way 'round.

2. Once you've found your spot, be sure it's relatively smooth. Sand and grass are the best surfaces, but you're not always going to be that lucky. Wherever you choose to pitch your tent, remember that rocks and roots under your sleeping pad magically become three hundred times bigger in the night.

3. You also need to think like water: Choose a site that will drain well, even in a downpour. If you know it's going to rain, be sure there are no slopes draining into your site.

4. Shade is a consideration, especially in summer. Waking up feeling like you're being cooked alive is generally not the best way to start your day.

5. It may seem obvious not to pitch your tent under a dead branch or tree, but plenty of campers have had to learn this the hard way. Don't be one of them! Likewise, keep an eye peeled for loose, rocky ledges, avalanche paths, and anything else that might come crashing down.

6. If it's windy, look for windbreaks. A row of stout trees or a large boulder can serve to stop the wind.

7. If possible, minimize your impact on nature by choosing a site that has already been used by other campers. No matter what, when you leave, pack out everything you packed in, and do your best to make it look as if you were never there.

HOW TO POOP IN THE WOODS

OK, SO MAYBE YOU'VE FIGURED THIS OUT by now, but everybody poops. No, really. Even on camping trips. Pooping without a toilet makes a lot of people uncomfortable, but worse, if done incorrectly, it can leave an unpleasant toxic pile at the side of a trail or campsite or leach into a pristine steam. Therefore, some frank talk about outdoor pooping etiquette is in order.

A cathole is the most widely accepted method of backcountry human waste disposal. Generally speaking, you dig a hole, do your business in it, and cover it up. Simple enough, right? Yes and no. Here are a few details to take note of.

SELECTING A SITE

Make sure you are two hundred feet from water sources, trails, and campsites. Select an inconspicuous site, untraveled by people. If you're camping with a group or for more than one night in the same place, disperse the catholes over a wide area. Sites with deep soil and good sunlight will aid in decomposition. Choose an elevated site where water won't collect when it rains, so the poop will decompose before it runs off into a water source.

DIGGING A HOLE

A small trowel carried in your pack is ideal when you need to dig a cathole, but a stick and/or a flat rock will work fine in a pinch. Dig the hole 6 to 8 inches deep and 4 to 6 inches in diameter.

CLEANING YOURSELF

Toilet paper is not recommended. If you choose to use it, double bag it and carry it out. Burning toilet paper is actually a common cause of forest fires, and please *do not* bury it. Sure, it seems like TP would easily decompose, but the evidence proves otherwise. Coming across someone else's toilet paper in the woods is really gross. As if you couldn't figure *that* out on your own.

Look, people have been pooping in the woods and cleaning themselves up for a long time, and TP is a relatively new invention. Smooth rocks or sticks, leaves (make sure they're leaves you know, to avoid poison ivy, stinging nettle, and such), a bundle of grass, and even snow all work just fine. A few options are even better: the soft, absorbent leaves of mullein were known as cowboy toilet paper, and large-leaf aster was the go-to for northeast lumberjacks.

THE BEST POOP JOKE EVER

A bear was taking a dump in the forest when a rabbit walked by. The bear said, "Hey rabbit, does poo stick to your fur?"

"No," replied the rabbit.

"Great," said the bear, as he picked up the rabbit and wiped his butt with him.

TOPPING IT OFF

When finished, the cathole should be topped off with the original dirt and disguised with native materials.

FINER POINTS

As with so many aspects of wilderness living, it's the little things that separate a master woods-pooper from a newbie. For instance, a MWP knows the trick of sitting on a log or boulder with his or her bum hanging over the edge above the carefully excavated cathole. If you close your eyes, don't think too hard, and manage to keep your balance, it's almost like being at home on the toilet.

Here's another technique we call the "tree hugger." Put your feet 4 to 6 inches from the base of a tree trunk and wrap your arms around the tree. Bend your knees and lean back so your butt isn't over your heels, while hanging onto the tree for support. (Just don't let go!)

Of course, there's always the ole stand-by: squat. This one's pretty self-explanatory; just keep your feet outta the way, get the drift?

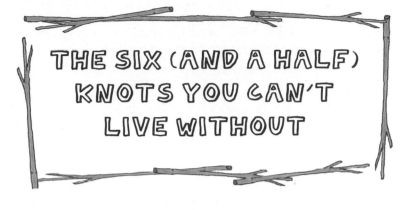

THE SIX (AND A HALF) KNOTS YOU CAN'T LIVE WITHOUT

MOST FOLKS STOP WORKING on their knot-tying skills after mastering their shoelaces. But the ubiquitous bunny-eared bow-knot isn't likely to keep your canoe from blowing off the roof of the car. Truth is, there are thousands of knots in the world, and you could spend the next ten years tangled up in rope trying to figure them all out. We're here to save you from that fate, with six (and a half) of the most versatile knots known to humankind.

1. SHEET BEND This is a bend knot, which means it ties two ropes together. It works even when the two ropes are of different size or material.

2. BOWLINE One of the most useful knots you can know. It forms a secure loop at the end of a line that is easy to tie and untie even after severe tension is applied.

3. TRUCKER'S HITCH This combination of knots allows a line to be pulled very tight. It is commonly used for securing loads on vehicles. Great for tying a canoe on top of a car.

4. CONSTRICTOR KNOT A useful knot to tie a bundle of items or the ends of bags. It grips itself and will not work loose. In fact, you might not be able to untie it!

5. CLOVE HITCH A simple knot to tie a rope to a post. It is easy to tie and untie. It is used to start and finish lashings (a series of wraps tying two poles together).

6. TAUT-LINE HITCH This knot can be slipped to tighten or loosen a line, then it holds fast under load. It is great for securing guylines on a tent or tarp.

6½. HALF HITCH Actually, the half hitch is just a regular overhand knot. Most often you will use two in succession. It is easy to tie, holds well under load, and is easy to loosen. Use a couple to tie rope to a tree or to your boat.

PROTECT YOUR GRUB

NO MATTER WHERE YOU CAMP, you're likely to have animal visitors, and it's probably not you they're visiting. It's our responsibility as campers to prevent wild animals from gaining access to human food—it disrupts their natural diet and over time creates dependence on people, which can become a safety threat for both the critters and us. In fact, bears that are too comfortable with humans are often killed. Fortunately, with just a little forethought and care, this is totally avoidable. For starters, follow these guidelines:

▶ Never leave food, trash, or other scented products inside your tent.

▶ Never leave "open" food unattended; jays, squirrels, and chipmunks can quickly snatch food in broad daylight, and other animals will come foraging at night.

▶ Keep odors at a distance. Set up your kitchen station well away from your tent so odors don't attract animals near where you sleep. Use only a small amount of unscented liquid soap. Better yet, don't use any soap at all.

▶ If possible, toss your rinse water over a rocky area a good distance from your campsite. But first, strain out food scraps and put them in your trash.

▶ Hang your food and your trash.

After you have protected your food from the bears and other wild animals, you might want to think about keeping perishables from spoiling. You probably don't have a fridge close at hand, so you're going to have to get creative.

If you have food that needs to be kept cool, or you just want to keep your drinkables cold, find a stream or river and use rocks to make a small half-circle dam. Anything you want to keep cool goes inside the dam; just be sure you've got your food in watertight and critter-proof containers!

No cold water source? The ground is a great insulator, so start digging. If you're storing food for long-term use, you will need to critter-proof it in some way (see the illustrations).

Finally, if all this seems like too much trouble, think about how relaxing it'll be to have a bear visit in the middle of the night. Not only that, but once he (or she) gets into your stash, there's probably not going to be much left over for you!

THIRTY-THREE WAYS TO USE A BANDANA

BANDANAS ARE ONE OF THE MOST VERSATILE and useful items you can carry in a pack, so make sure you always have at least a couple with you. They should be 100 percent cotton or they won't be useful for many of the following applications:

1. Handkerchief. (We know, we know ... who woulda thought?!?)

2. Fold up and tie around your head to keep sweat out of your eyes.

3. First aid (sling, bandage, wrap around snow for ice pack, stop the flow of blood, tie on a splint).

4. Potholder.

5. Pasta strainer.

6. Salad spinner. (Put washed greens on it, fold up the corners, and swing it around your head until your lettuce is properly dizzy.)

7. Tie things to your bike.

8. Emergency pack strap repair.

9. Tie a knot in each corner and wear it as a hat.

10. Tie two together for a belt.

11. Blindfold for games.

12. Wrap around a fire-heated stone and place in the foot of your sleeping bag on cold nights.

13. Towel or washcloth.

14. Tie things to your pack.

15. Wrap up a sandwich.

16. Cover exposed food to protect it from insects.

17. Tie pant legs closed to keep out ticks, chiggers, or other pesky insects of your region.

18. Tuck under hat to hang down neck as sun protection.

19. Tie opposing corners together for a berry basket.

20. Clean camera or binocular or glasses lenses.

21. Trail or campsite marker.

22. Rip in strips to make cordage.

23. Bind a stone inside and use for weight to toss a line over a limb.

24. Padding under a strap when carrying a heavy load.

25. Cover your face from smoke around the campfire.

26. Smoke signals.

27. Signal flag.

28. Distract a charging animal.

29. Patch a hole.

30. Net minnows for bait.

31. Fly swatter.

32. Napkin.

33. Toilet paper (only *after* you've used it as a napkin).

BUILD THE PERFECT FIRE FOR COOKING STUFF

ANY OLD FIRE CAN KEEP YOU WARM, light up the night, and burn a marshmallow, but a cooking fire is a different beast. The key is, for successful cooking you don't want *fire,* you want glowing hot coals, or "embers," to provide lots of heat to cook your food as opposed to burning the heck out of it with flames. For any fire, start with the following preparations:

1. First, think about the location. If your campsite has a designated fire ring, use it. If not, select a fire pit site away from trees and bushes, and away from your tent and gear, for that matter. Don't set up on grass, particularly dead grass. You want bare ground. Clear an area of all plant matter. Circle it with rocks to keep the fire contained. Keep water nearby (and use plenty of it to put out your fire when you go to sleep or leave your camp).

2. Next, you'll need to gather wood, three kinds: tinder, kindling, and bigger stuff. These should all have one thing in common; they should be *dry*. Any wood you collect should break easily; if it bends, it is too wet or "green" (that is, too fresh). The other thing each kind of wood will have in common is that you'll probably need a lot more of it than you think!

3. Make piles of each kind of wood you collect. Your tinder pile should consist of stuff that catches fire easily but burns fast. Think dry grass and leaves, shredded dry bark, dry wood shavings. Tinder material is the firestarter that gets things going. After that, you'll be needing small kindling; look for pieces of wood that range in diameter from mouse tail to pencil. Once you have the small stuff blazing, you'll need bigger fuel to build a bigger fire; branches that are about the diameter of your arm will be ideal for that.

When you're ready to cook, you can match your fire to your meal. For instance, if you only want to heat up leftovers or quickly boil some water, you don't need to build a serious campfire and then wait an hour for it to burn down to embers. Put a pile of tinder in the middle of the fire pit. Set up some of your "mouse tails" around the tinder in a teepee shape and some of your "pencils" around that. Light the tinder and let it all burn for a few minutes, until the teepee collapses—providing a spot to nestle your pot into. If you need more heat, add more twigs and branches around the pot. It won't keep you very warm and it won't cook a bison on a spit, but it is just the thing for a cup of hot chocolate.

However, say you've got a hankerin' for the aforementioned bison. Start with the same teepee setup as above but make it a little bigger and add some larger kindling. Once you get this burning, start adding some of the bigger fuel by making a stepped pyramid of the branches. Place two branches perpendicular to each other on either side of the teepee and two more across the first two but going the other way. Alternate in this manner until you have four or five courses. On the last course lay a few extras branches across, closing in the top of the pyramid. Let this burn down to chunky embers while you prepare your meal. This makes it much easier to control the heat, since you can move the coals to where you need them. In fact, you can even make multiple "burners" of different heat intensities by strategically piling your coals: a small pile for a pot of simmering rice, and a big ole pile to put the finishing touches on something meaty.

BREAD ON A STICK

BREAD COOKED ON A STICK IS A FUN and filling camping snack that can be made in 15 minutes, and probably less if you work fast. It is a variation on an unleavened campfire bread ("unleavened" means it doesn't use yeast or sourdough starter to "rise") called bannock, which has been filling adventurer's bellies for over a thousand years. The ingredients are simple, it is easy to cook, and there are lots of ways to vary the taste (see the sidebar).

Any bread recipe will work, as well as just flour and water. That said, here's our favorite. For ease of traveling, we pack the dry ingredients in a Ziploc bag, and add the water and fat at camp.

2 cups flour
⅓ cup butter, lard, bacon grease, or olive oil
2 teaspoons baking powder
½ teaspoon salt
About 1 cup water

1. Get a fire going well before you're hungry (see page 82); that way, you'll have hot coals to cook over when the dough is mixed up.

2. Mix the dry ingredients with the fat and as much water as you need to make dough. Make sure to mix everything really well, then divide the dough into twelve balls.

3. Cut a stiff, green (that is, live, not dry) stick and roll a dough ball between your palms until it's about half an inch thick and looks like a snake. Wrap the snake in a spiral down the top part of the stick as shown in the illustration.

4. Cook the dough over the hot coals, turning it frequently until cooked through or until you're so hungry you can't wait any longer, whichever comes first.

Hot tip: This bread can also be made in a greased skillet. Just flatten out the dough balls, cook for a few minutes, then flip to be sure they're cooked through.

NOW WE'RE TALKIN'!

⟶

Add in some or all(!) of these delicious extras:

Raisins or other dried fruit	**Nuts**	**Parmesan cheese and herbs** (probably make a separate batch for these!)
Honey	**Chopped bacon**	
	Apples	
Maple sugar		
	Coconut	
Cinnamon		**Sundried tomatoes**
	Chocolate chips	
Berries		
	Cocoa	

MAKE A FEAST WITHOUT ANY DISHES TO WASH!

JUST BECAUSE YOU DON'T WANT to lug a bunch of pots on your camping trip—and who does?—there's no need to resort to a cold can of beans. Actually, there are lots of ways to cook over a fire with things you can find around your campsite; no cumbersome pots necessary. Here are four ideas to get you started.

1. It doesn't get much simpler than this: a hot flat rock strategically placed inside your fire ring can double as a skillet. Just a minor detail: a rock full of moisture can explode like a grenade when placed in or over a fire. There's no need to be paranoid, but you'll want to dress in full body armor before you... OK, OK, just kidding. Truth is, a wet rock can explode, but it has to be pretty darn saturated. A rained-on rock is fine—just leave those river rocks where they are.

You can fry anything you want on top of a hot rock... meat, fish, vegetables, eggs, whatever you've got. Slick trick: Lay four slices of bacon in a square, let them cook until the underside is done, then flip them over, keeping your square. Now crack a couple eggs in the middle of the square so the bacon keeps them contained.

2. Wrapping meat, fish, or veggies to cook in green (fresh) leaves is an ancient practice, and a great way to connect with your inner hunter-gatherer. The moisture in the leaves helps steam the food and prevents it from burning. Make sure the leaves overlap. If they are skinny leaves like cattail or ramps, just spiral them around the food. This works better for slabs of meat and fish than for pieces of meat or veggies. For those, choose big leaves and a skinny leaf or wet twine to tie it up. Place the leaf packet directly on the coals or next to the fire. It gives food a smoky, grilled flavor that takes on the aroma of whatever kind of leaf you use.

WILD LEAF OPTIONS

Sumac	Burdock	Cherry
Ramps (wild onions)	Oak	Walnut
Wild garlic	Cattails	Chestnut
Nettles	Maple	

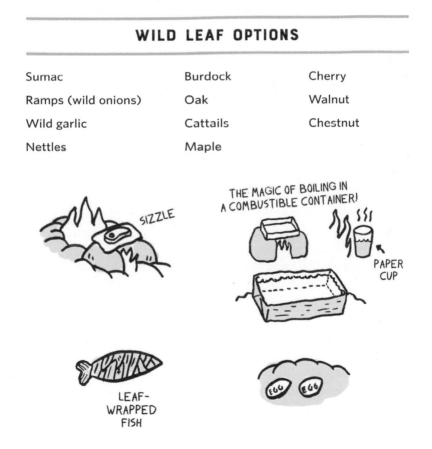

SIZZLE

THE MAGIC OF BOILING IN A COMBUSTIBLE CONTAINER!

PAPER CUP

LEAF-
WRAPPED
FISH

3. It may seem counterintuitive, but you can actually boil water in many containers that you would normally think don't mix with fire, such as a folded bark container (like on page 134) or—get this— even a paper cup. It works because water boils at 212 degrees, which is below the ignition point of the container holding it.

4. If you've got a hankering for hard-boiled eggs, just pull some warm ashes and embers to the side of your campfire and bury your eggs in them. You'll have soft-boiled eggs in about 10 minutes and hard-boiled in 15 to 20 minutes, depending on the temperature of the ashes.

OUTDOOR FIRST AID

AS WITH MOST OF OUR OTHER NEEDS, we have gotten used to relying on commercial products to treat even the most minor aches and pains. Truth is, many of today's common medicines are derived from plants. For instance, the active component in aspirin is acetyl salicylic acid, which is a derivative of the compound salicin. Guess what? Salicin is found in many plants and trees.

Once upon a time, the medicinal uses of most common plants were known by even young children, who were perfectly able to treat their own bug bites, cuts, rashes, and scratches. Major or life-threatening wounds or illnesses were usually delegated to a community's healer, who was versed in the more intricate and complicated applications of herbs, along with other forms of traditional healing. These practitioners were available to everyone—no health insurance necessary—and were mutually supported by their community, relying on that community to provide them with resources such as food, clothing, and firewood. If this sounds like a sweet deal, remember that healers were directly accountable to their neighbors for the outcome of their work. If they were trying to get rid of the wart on your grandmother's toe and it moved to her nose and got three times as big, it was a little embarrassing to run into her at the village feast. This face-to-face accountability eliminated the need for laws surrounding health care. Unfortunately, much of our traditional healing wisdom has been lost to the modern, for-profit health-care industry.

Still, it's not too late for us to regain at least some basic knowledge of the healing properties of plants in order to be able to treat our own minor afflictions, whether we're at home or out adventuring in the wild. Here are three common plants that are easily identified and can offer natural, effective relief from the irritation of small aches and pains. You don't need to live in the sticks or be on a camping trip to find these healing plants; they're common in lawns, parks, and playgrounds. Just be sure they aren't sprayed with pesticides!

Note: Before you begin, please check out the sidebar on page xiii for tips on safely and respectfully harvesting from the wild. Once you've got all this sussed out, you're good to go.

▶ PLANTAIN, known as the "Band-Aid plant," is one of the best wound healers around. It typically begins blooming in June, sporting small cattail-like stalks of seeds that shoot up from a green rosette of leaves that hug the ground. The leaves have five parallel veins running the length of each leaf.

Not only does plantain increase the speed of healing, but it also relieves pain, stops bleeding, draws out foreign matter, stops itching, prevents and halts allergic reactions from bee stings, kills bacteria, and reduces swelling. According to rumor, it'll even do your homework and take out the trash. Use it on sprains, cuts, insect bites, rashes, boils, bruises, chapped and cracked lips, rough hands, burns, and the like.

Simply pick a leaf, crush it or chew it up, and apply to the affected area. Plantain leaf can also be chewed to help alleviate the pain from a toothache.

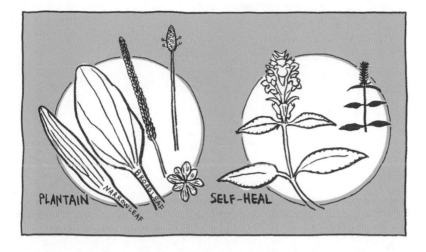

CHICKWEED is a mild but very effective plant known for its cooling and soothing properties. This small, succulent plant has a smooth stem with a line of hair running along it like a horse's mane and has a tiny white flower with ten petals. It can be harvested in abundance in the spring and again in the fall.

Chickweed is particularly good for dry and inflamed skin conditions such as eczema, psoriasis, and poison ivy rash, as well as for minor bites, cuts, scrapes, burns, and bee stings. As with plantain, it has a drawing action useful for removing splinters and the stingers of bees. Extract its juices by crushing it between your fingers, then apply it to the affected area.

SELF-HEAL is a scentless perennial mint and one of the great unsung healers of the plant world. It is a low, creeping plant with a compact clump of small violet flowers on a solitary square stem. The leaves and flowers contain more antioxidants than any other plant ever tested, and it's a powerful anti-inflammatory. It also helps stop the flow of blood and fuses the edges of a wound back together. Crush the leaves and apply directly to the wound.

MAKE YOUR OWN FRUIT LEATHER

THE CORPORATE FOOD INDUSTRY wants us to believe that neon blue and green "energy" drinks and prepackaged, sugared-up snacks are the fuel of champions.

But we don't have to take the bait. In fact, you can easily make your own nutritious snacks to keep you chugging during all sorts of adventures, from short hikes to long camping trips. We like drying because it's one of the best ways to preserve foods while maintaining essential nutrients. Plus, dried fruit takes up about 600 percent less space in your pack than fresh and weighs hardly anything. Best of all, these snacks taste wicked good and are super simple to make.

You can source your fruit wherever and however works best for you, but it's particularly satisfying to forage wild berries or apples. You could also visit a local orchard or berry farm to pick your own.

Fruit (see individual directions for amounts)

Sweetener (optional)

Cinnamon and nutmeg (optional)

A rimmed baking sheet (any size will do)

PREPPING THE FRUIT

Follow the instructions below for preparing the various fruits, then scrape the fruit onto a rimmed baking sheet and follow the instructions for drying.

BERRIES

Fruits with lots of moisture (think blueberries, strawberries, raspberries, and so on) do best if they are cooked down and thickened before drying. Put several quarts of berries in a heavy-bottom pan and cook on very low heat, mashing them down from time to time until they thicken. Add sweetener if you like.

APPLES

Grind cored apples, with or without their peels, in a food processor. If you like, add sweetener or spice (or both) to taste. For a real treat, grind some nuts in with the apples, or just add a dollop or two of nut butter. (Raw apples prepared like this make for a crunchier snack, as opposed to the usual chewy fruit leather.)

Applesauce, whether homemade or store-bought, can also be dried for fruit leather.

BANANAS

Got brown bananas? Don't toss 'em! Mash 'em and dry 'em. It's that simple.

DRYING THE LEATHER

For drying, you need airflow and just a bit of heat—too much heat, and you'll cook the fruit, which is not what you want. If you live somewhere hot and dry, you're set. Put your fruit-filled baking sheet out in the sun, cover it with cheesecloth to keep the flies away, and leave it to dry until you can gently lift a corner of the dried fruit "sheet" and flip the whole thing over to finish drying.

If you live somewhere cooler and more humid, you'll have to work a little harder. It will take several sunny days in a row to dry a tray, and you will have to bring it in at night so as not to lose all you gained during the day. Propping a window over the tray to increase heat will help, or you can leave the tray inside near a large south-facing window on several sunny days. We often resort to finishing our leather in the oven on its lowest setting with the door propped open a crack. When the sheet is dry enough to hold together, flip it over and put it directly on the oven rack until any tackiness is gone. An actual food dehydrator is the easiest option and has the most consistent results. Either way, let the leather cool and then rip it into whatever size pieces you want. Store them in a jar or Ziploc bag, and next time you're heading out the door, grab a handful for the road or trail.

MAKE A DAKOTA FIRE HOLE

MAYBE YOU'RE NOT INTO CHOPPING firewood, or maybe you're camping in a spot where gathering firewood isn't an option, or maybe you just want to make something really cool. No matter what, a little cooker called a Dakota fire hole will put hot food or drink in your belly with just a handful of twigs, pinecones, and even bark. It was named after the Native American tribe that invented it hundreds of years ago, which means you can make it without any modern manufactured supplies.

If the wind is light, and you can't tell which direction it's coming from, here's a neat trick. You might have seen people put their finger in their mouth and then hold it up to test the direction of the wind. You might have even thought they looked a little silly, but the joke's on you, because this technique actually works quite well. The key is to wet your whole finger, not just one side. You'll know the direction of the wind by noticing what side of your finger feels coldest.

Not only is the Dakota fire hole ridiculously efficient, it's non-polluting as well. You'll notice it produces very little smoke; the less smoke, the more complete the combustion, and therefore, the less pollution.

HOW TO DO IT

1. Remove a plug of sod about 8 inches in diameter and set it aside for replacement when you are finished. Dig a hole about 10 inches deep. About 4 inches down, start to widen the hole by several inches all the way around.

2. Figure out which way the wind is blowing (see sidebar), and about 10 inches away, in the direction of the wind, dig another hole, again saving the sod plug and soil for replacement. This hole needs to be about 6 inches in diameter on an angle, sloping toward the first hole so it meets at the bottom of the first hole (see the illustration).

3. Make a rim of flat rocks around the vertical hole to put your pot on, but be sure air can still flow into the hole.

4. Clear away flammable material in the area.

5. Fill the pit with dry kindling material and light the fire. Slowly add sticks to make a strong, hot fire. Once the fire is going, put your pot on the rock rim. If your pot is too small, just lay some green (meaning live, not the color) branches across the hole in a parallel fashion to support your pot. The fire is then fed from the angled hole. You don't need anything bigger than twigs to feed it, due to its incredible efficiency.

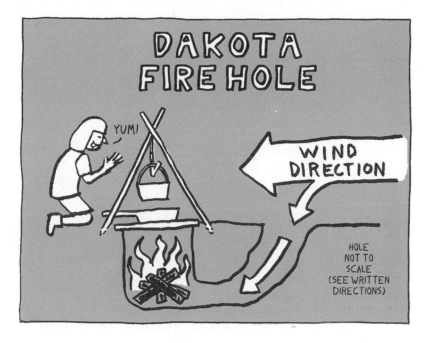

HOW IT WORKS

As hot air from the fire exits through the top of the fire pit, suction is created, drawing fresh air down through the tunnel and into the base of the fire. This brings in plenty of oxygen—just what's needed for combustion. As the fire burns, a cycle develops: The hotter the fire gets, the more air is drawn down into the pit, making the fire hotter still, which means more air is drawn into the pit, which means the fire is getting . . . yeah, you get the point.

When you are finished with the stove, just fill in the holes with the original soil and top it off with the sod plug. This puts out the fire and leaves little trace of your presence. And that's the way it's supposed to be.

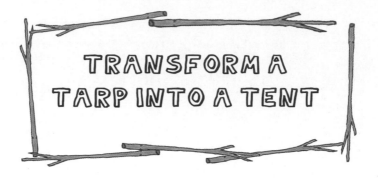

TRANSFORM A TARP INTO A TENT

THAT TARP YOU'RE CARRYING in your "ten essentials" kit (see page 64) can be transformed into a tent in a whole bunch of ways! Here's a basic one:

STUFF YOU'LL NEED

One or two tarps (8 by 10 feet is a good size for one person)

Paracord (lightweight nylon rope available from hardware stores) or other strong rope, at least 50 feet

A saw (optional)

HOW TO DO IT

➤ Find an area with two trees around 10 feet apart, depending on the size of your tarp.

➤ Use the paracord to tie a pole (a dead sapling is fine) horizontally between the two trees, about 4 or 5 feet from the ground (again, depending

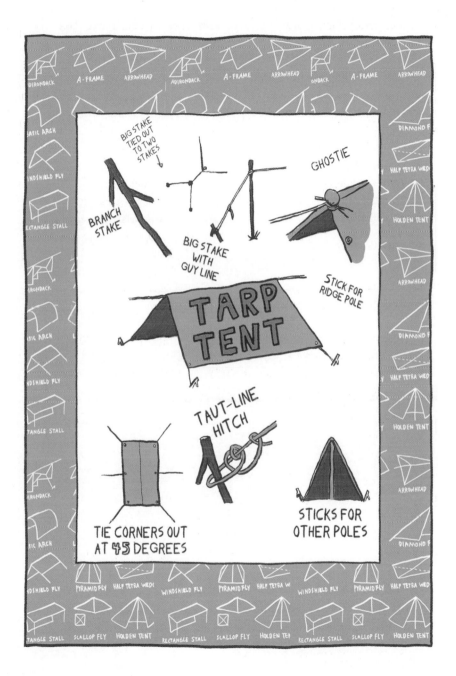

on the size of the tarp). A less-rigid alternative is to use a taut-line hitch (see page 74) to tie a piece of parachute cord around one tree roughly four or five feet from the ground. Run the line to the other tree and tie that end off as well. Make sure the line is tight to prevent any sagging, or use sticks for prop poles as seen in the illustration.

▶ Throw the tarp over the pole or line so the middle of the tarp hangs over the cord.

▶ Use more paracord to pull out each corner taut and tie off to trees or stakes in the ground.

▶ If you have a second tarp, you can put that on the ground. Otherwise, just use a camp pad and sleep tight!

If your tarp's grommet holes rip out, or they are just in the wrong place, make a "ghostie" by wrapping a rock in the edge of the tarp and tying the rope around the rock.

STRING UP A CHICKEN

BACK WHEN COOKING IN THE FIREPLACE was our ancestors' only option, a chicken roasting at the hearth had to be turned constantly to avoid uneven cooking. Having someone sit there and turn a spit that the chicken was skewered on was problematic, not only because it was rather boring but also because there was water to haul, crops to tend, and maybe even a cow or twenty to milk.

So, someone came up with the ingenious solution of hanging the chicken from a piece of string attached to a hook above the fire. Once the string is weighted down by the meat, the chicken begins turning all on its lonesome, as if by magic. After a while it slows down and stops, hanging motionless, and then, somehow, begins turning again in the opposite direction. Periodically, it will stop turning on its own, but a slight touch sets it back in motion. The list of instructions makes this look more daunting than it is; that's only because there are a lot of little details that make this work.

STUFF YOU'LL NEED

Tripod	Salt	Two wooden or
Fire	Pepper	metal skewers
String	Olive oil	
Whole chicken	Drip pan	

THE TRIPOD

To do this over a campfire, you will need to set up a tripod to act as the hook. Three green (meaning fresh, not dry) saplings about wrist thick tied tightly together a few inches down from the top and spread in a triangle around your fire pit will do the trick. Metal rods, such as rebar (the stuff that goes in concrete), tied at the top is also a good option if you're doing this in your backyard. The taller your tripod, the longer the string can be, and the longer the string is, the longer the chicken will turn without being given a push. At a minimum, the poles should be 6 feet tall.

Position the tripod so the chicken will hang at the edge of the fire, making use of as much heat as possible without being in the flames.

THE FIRE

You need to get a good fire going for this one. The air around the area where you are roasting the bird is like the air of an oven; the hotter it is, the faster it will roast. So, get a fire going at least an hour before you want to cook (see "Build the Perfect Fire for Cooking Stuff" on page 82). There should be a substantial bed of hot coals (maybe six good-sized logs' worth), with several more logs still producing good flames, that will eventually be embers you can drag closer to the chicken. Place the tripod so the chicken will hang close to the fire but not directly in it. Make sure you have some dry kindling and logs on hand to boost the heat if need be.

THE STRING

Use a natural fiber string that is as thin as possible while still able to support the weight of the bird. The thinness of the string will also impact the length of time the bird will spin before needing a push.

Cut a piece of string about the length of the tripod legs. Put a 1-inch diameter loop in one end and tie the other end to the tripod intersection so the loop hangs down about 1½ feet from the ground.

You will also need a piece of string for a handle to hold the chicken and to make it easy to flip it over or to remove it from the long string. This piece should have a 1-inch loop at either end and be about 18 inches long, but the length will vary as you figure out how close to the fire the meat needs to hang. You could make a couple of different lengths and try them out or wait and get a more precise measurement after everything else is set up.

THE BIRD

Rinse the whole chicken and pat it dry. Rub the skin with olive oil, salt, and pepper, and truss the chicken. This just means to tie the legs and wings close to the body, which helps make the bird as compact as possible for more even roasting. When trussed, the whole thing should look a bit like an egg, which is sort of funny, because eggs come from . . . ah, forget about it. Stick a skewer through from thigh to thigh and another one from wing to wing. The skewers should be parallel to each other, go through the center of the bird, and stick out on each side by an inch or two.

Take one of the string handles and hook the loops on each side of one of the skewers so you can lift up the bird with the handle. It should hang pretty straight; you can reposition the skewer if it tilts too much. Test the second skewer in the same way and put the string back on the first one.

Put the chicken in a bowl (string still attached) and carry it to the fire. Take one side of the handle string off the skewer, pass it through the loop on the string coming off the tripod, and hook it back onto the other side of the skewer (it can be *really* helpful to have a helper in this!). Lower the bowl so the chicken is hanging. Check the distance from the fire, and adjust it with different-sized handle strings so it hangs 6 to 8 inches above the fire. Place a drip pan on the ground under the bird with a cup of water in it. Push the loops of the handle flush against the bird and give it a gentle push to start it spinning.

Add water to the drip pan when needed to keep the drippings from burning.

Flip the chicken to the other skewer at least once while cooking. The bird is done when a thermometer reads 180 degrees in the thigh. This could take an hour or much longer, depending on the fire. You can always speed it along by goosing the fire with some kindling. The first few times you do this it will be nearly impossible to judge when it will be done, so give yourself plenty of leeway, have some snacks on hand, and know the end result is worth the wait. It is absolutely the best chicken we've ever eaten.

When the bird is done, remove it from the string and put it on a plate to rest. If after 10 minutes of resting it hasn't jumped up and run away, dig in.

BRUSH YOUR TEETH WITH A STICK

IF YOU THOUGHT forgetting to pack your toothbrush was an excuse to skip your nightly ritual, think again, 'cause it's totally possible to clean your chompers with nothing more than a humble stick. Heck, there's probably a million and one toothbrushes hiding in plain sight within a hundred feet of your tent. Besides, you don't really want to end up with your teeth all rotted out like your Uncle Eldridge, do you?

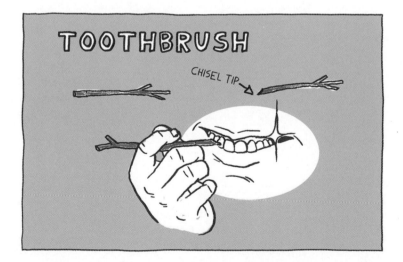

HOW TO DO IT

1. Find a dry stick about ⅛ to ³⁄₁₆ inches in diameter and 8 to 12 inches long.

2. Grab it at each end with your thumbs sticking out and pointing toward the middle of the stick. Your thumbs should be a few inches apart. Snap the stick in half, and likely as not you'll end up with a chisel shape on the end. If you don't end up with a good shape, use your knife to fix it up. That shape is perfect for scraping the flat sides of your teeth.

3. Working from the back all the way around your mouth, scrape each tooth on the front and back. Wood is flexible, so you can use quite a bit of pressure— just be careful of poking into your gums. If you say "ow!" and start hopping up and down on one foot, that's a good indication to back off.

4. After the flat surfaces are all shined up, make yourself a slightly pokey stick to clean out the biting surfaces and the cracks between the teeth. This may sound time-consuming, but once you get some practice, it goes fast, and you won't believe how good your teeth feel afterward. In fact, you might start forgetting your toothbrush a whole lot more often.

PART THREE

MAKE REALLY COOL STUFF THAT'S ACTUALLY USEFUL

WILLOW BASKET

BASKETRY IS ONE OF THE OLDEST CRAFTS in human history. For thousands of years baskets served as indispensable objects in every culture and are still employed by millions of people around the world on a daily basis. Here's how to make one for yourself.

Unless you live in Australia (sorry, mates), there's willow growing on your continent, and that's good, because a big part of the fun of making things from willow is tromping around creeks, rivers, and other boggy areas on the hunt for prime specimens. Consult a tree identification book or do an internet search to see what you're looking for. There are a whole bunch of willow species, but not all of them are suitable for baskets. If the young branches can be bent at 90 degrees without breaking, you are good to go.

Harvest willow when it's dormant, which is any time after the leaves have fallen and before growth starts in the spring; this is generally November through March. You'll want to cut the rods when temps are above freezing to prevent the wood from splintering.

Cut the present year's growth (these will be the smallest shoots) so that the shoot is flexible enough to weave with. A good test is if it wraps around your wrist without snapping. If you can't find willow, any species that passes the wrist-wrap test can be used to make your basket.

STUFF YOU'LL NEED

Approximately thirty (more to choose from is always nice) willow shoots, no fatter than the diameter of a pencil, 3 feet long and free of branching

Pruning shears

A knife

A clothespin (optional)

A branch or broom handle (optional)

HOW TO DO IT

1. Lay three of the longer shoots that are thickest in diameter crossing each other at their middles to create a six-armed star. Cut a fourth shoot (of similar size) in half and set aside.

2. From your pile, grab one of the smallest-diameter shoots. With the narrow end, begin at the center of the star and weave over one arm and under the next, going around the center of the star once. Unless you have four or five hands, this beginning part can be tricky. Don't be afraid to have a buddy help you hold things in place. A clothespin can also be really useful.

Hot tip: Before you use a piece of willow for weaving, it really helps to "condition" it to bend the way you want it to. A branch or broom handle works great to wrap the shoots around to break some of the fibers and encourage it to be more flexible.

3. Notice that if you kept going like this you would be going under the same arms you went under on the first round and over the same arms you went over on the first round. This is what the half shoot is for. Stick it into the weaving to become the seventh arm, and continue the over-under pattern.

4. When you run out of one rod just add another one, overlapping them by a couple of arms. Always splice butts to butts or tips to tips. Pay attention to keeping the spacing even between the arms, as they have a way of sliding around and getting too close to one another.

Alert: Here is a good time to say *do not get discouraged*. As our basketmaker friend says, there is always an "ugly basket" stage, and maybe even two. Just keep going and trying to pull things tight. Gaps can get filled in later—and no matter what, your basket will hold *something*. Maybe not berries, but definitely a grapefruit.

5. Continue weaving the base until it is about 6 inches in diameter. It can be less if you want a smaller basket, but don't go bigger because you would need to add more "arms" to make a tight weave.

6. When the base is finished, the arms need to be "upset" (in basketry terms). To make a hinge in the rod and help it to fold up smoothly, use this little trick: Take your knife and stick the tip into but not through an arm at the outer edge of the base to make a short, vertical slit. Keep your knife in the slit and simultaneously twist the knife a quarter turn and fold the arm up 90 degrees. Let the arm come back down and do the same thing to the other six.

7. Fold all the arms up to meet at the top, and use a thin piece of willow to tie them together.

8. Start weaving a shoot under and over around the basket, working your way up the sides. Pay attention to what shape basket you want. Depending on how tight you pull the weavers, the sides will slope out or be more vertical. Keep splicing in new shoots, butt to butt and tip to tip, pulling the weavers tight and pushing down to close the gaps between the rows of weaving, until your basket is as tall as you want it, making sure to leave 6 inches of arm to make the rim.

9. To make the rim, kink each arm just above where the weaving ended, so they fold down to the right. Start with one arm and fold it down to the right, going in front of the next two arms and behind the third one, and out to the front. The next arm to the right is woven in the same manner, in front of two arms, behind the next and out to the front, lying on top of the previous arm. (See the illustration.) Continue until there are three arms still standing. These are taken down in the same pattern but will have to be threaded into place under the arms that were taken down first. If you get confused, look back at a completed arm and follow it as a model. Remember that each arm lies on top of the one before it.

10. Trim off any ends that are sticking out anywhere on the basket. Cut them on an angle so they lie as flat as possible. Yay! You have a perfectly functional basket. If you are bothered by gaps in the base, you can weave shoots in wherever you want. If you want a handle, go on to step 11.

11. To make a handle for your basket, choose two shoots of the largest diameter you have. From the butt end, cut them to the approximate size you want for your handle plus twice the height of your basket. Push the butt end of one down through the rows of weaving, right next to an arm, all the way to the base. Bend it up over the basket to form a handle. Push the other end of the shoot down through all the rows of weaving, next to the arm on the opposite side of the basket. Do the same thing with the other shoot on the other side of the arm, but reverse the direction of the butt and tip ends. As you are bending this one up over the basket, twist it around the first handle piece a few times. That could be it, or you could twist a few narrower pieces around the handle and push them down into the weave.

Truth: Your second basket will be better than your first, your third better than your second, and so on. We promise.

SHEPHERD'S SLING

SLINGS WERE FIRST USED thousands of years ago for hunting and as a combat weapon. They were small and portable and, in the hands of a skilled slinger, accurate and deadly. In fact, slings are so lethal that they were used in war into the 1700s and were what cavalry men used for long-range hits. A skilled slinger was extremely valuable to an army. The preferred ammo was smooth stones about the size and shape of a small egg, but clay and lead missiles were eventually manufactured. Occasionally, they were even inscribed with messages such as "take that!" or "ouch!" (This sounds like a joke, but it's true!)

Eventually, of course, the sling was replaced by gunpowder and then was pretty much forgotten—except by a few tribal herdsmen who still use this elegantly simple device to scare off predators, giving it its other name of shepherd's sling. Now, you can help revive this ancient tool and bust some targets up in the process. Basically, a sling is a bit of string and a small piece of cloth or leather. It is super easy to make, and the ammo is free for the finding. It'll take a while to get the hang of it (practice in large, open spaces, away from windows and people). But once you become proficient, you'll be amazed at the accuracy that's possible.

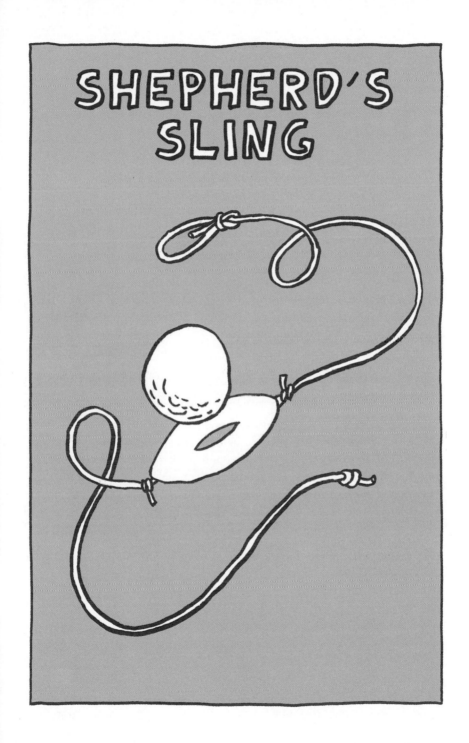

STUFF YOU'LL NEED

A piece of leather approximately 6 inches by 2½ inches. Although leather is ideal, in fact any heavy-duty cloth will do.

A 5-foot piece of string. This can be nylon, cotton, paracord, homemade cordage (see page 139), or even a couple of shoe laces—just about anything will work.

HOW TO MAKE IT

1. Cut the leather or cloth into a football shape to make the sling pocket.

2. Make a hole on either side of the pocket, about half an inch from the edge.

3. Cut the string in two pieces, with one about 4 inches longer than the other.

4. Use a bowline knot (see page 73) to attach a piece of string to each side of the pocket.

5. With another bowline, form a finger loop at the free end of the longer piece of string. The loop should be just big enough for your middle finger to slide in easily.

6. Make a knot at the end of the other piece of string, keeping the two lengths even.

HOW TO USE IT

Once your sling is made, things get fun and a bit tricky.

▶ Find some roundish stones a little smaller than a golf ball.

▶ Slip the loop over the middle finger of your dominant hand, and pinch the knot between your thumb and forefinger of the same hand.

▶ Put the stone in the pocket and adjust the strings so the pocket is cradling the stone level.

▶ Try some easy overhand throws, releasing the knotted line as the pocket reaches the top of its orbit. This should propel the rock forward. The key word here is "should."

▶ Once you feel more comfortable, you can try doing a few overhead circles before you release the knot, to generate more power.

▶ There are many other styles of throwing, including underhand, overhead, and helicopter-style. Feel free to play around, but don't forget that windows are expensive and that you really, truly can hurt someone with your new tool.

DEBRIS-HUT FORT

A WELL-BUILT DEBRIS SHELTER made of nothing more than sticks and leaves can last for years with just a little maintenance and can keep you warm, even on the coldest winter nights. It sounds totally crazy, we know, and we'd never have believed it ourselves if we hadn't tried it.

Follow the same rules for finding the best spot to pitch your tent (see page 66), plus one more that is rather important: make sure the site has a lot of debris around!

STUFF YOU'LL NEED

Sticks

Leaves

Imagination

Two hands

Two trees for breaking sticks between

HOW TO DO IT

1. Make a well-packed, 6-inch-thick, bed-sized pile of leaves and other soft debris. This is partly because it is more comfortable than the bare ground but also because the ground will steal your precious body heat. Test the bed for comfort and size, but don't fall asleep—you're not finished yet!

2. With your bed established, it's time to make the frame for your shelter. The sticks you use should be sturdy and about 3 to 4 inches in diameter; dead ones are fine. You will need two forked sticks that are about belly button height and one for the ridge pole that is a little less than two times your full height; it is possible to break even a thick branch to a precise length by sticking it between two trees that are close together and prying until you hear a satisfying "snap." Angle the forked sticks to form a triangle with the ground at one end of your bed so they meet at the top to form a notch. Lay the other, longer stick in the notch and angle it down to the ground over your bed, as seen in the illustration. There should only be enough room to barely roll over in the shelter. Since you will be relying on your body heat for warmth, too big can mean too cold.

3. Once the frame is up, start adding the "ribs" of the shelter by leaning more sticks up against the ridge pole. Any straightish sticks that are from 1 to 3 inches in diameter will do, but they should not exceed the height of the ridge pole, or they will provide a channel for rain. They should be spaced a few inches apart from each other all the way down the pole.

4. Add smaller branchy sticks on top and between the ribs until you have a good layer covering each side.

5. Now is the time to go nuts with fluffier debris. Leaves, pine needles, and dried grass are great for insulation. An effective way to gather a lot is to lay your jacket or shirt on the ground and move around it in a circular fashion, scraping leaves onto it like a dog covering his . . . oh, never mind. When you have a good pile, fold up the corners, carry it to your frame, and spread it on top. Repeat until you have a layer over the entire roof. The depth of the leaves should come to somewhere between your elbow and your armpit when you stick your arm into the layer. Don't skimp! The colder and wetter the weather, the thicker you'll want your roof.

6. Use forked sticks and cross pieces to make a doorframe and entrance tunnel (igloo-style), about knee height, which will serve to keep debris, snow, and rain out of your space and minimize wind infiltration. Top it all with sticks and leaves as you did with the main structure.

7. Finally, make an insulating door plug by filling your shirt or jacket or backpack with leaves one last time and pulling it behind you to close off the doorframe. If it is really cold, pile leaves all around you inside the shelter, too. If you use enough, you can even leave your sleeping bag at home!

BIRCH BARK KNIFE SHEATH

THE BARK OF WHITE BIRCH is the traditional sheath material of Scandinavia. The method described in this chapter is a slick way to make a quickie sheath for anything: knife, scissors, chisel, or what-have-you. These creations are a little addictive; once you make one, you'll find yourself looking for other things that could use a sheath. The pieces of bark needed are relatively small; just keep your eyes open for downed white birch trees, pieces of bark on the ground, or bark on wood in firewood piles. See page 134 for more info on white birch (also known as paper birch), and read the section titled "Harvesting Paper Birch Bark" (page 137) if you need to take bark from a tree. Alternatively, you could use thin cardboard (cereal boxes work well).

STUFF YOU'LL NEED

A piece of birch bark four times the length of your knife blade and ³⁄₈ inch wider

A ¼-inch-thick strip of the longest piece of birch bark you have (a 1¼- by 4-inch sheath takes about 26 inches of weaver strip), or two shorter pieces

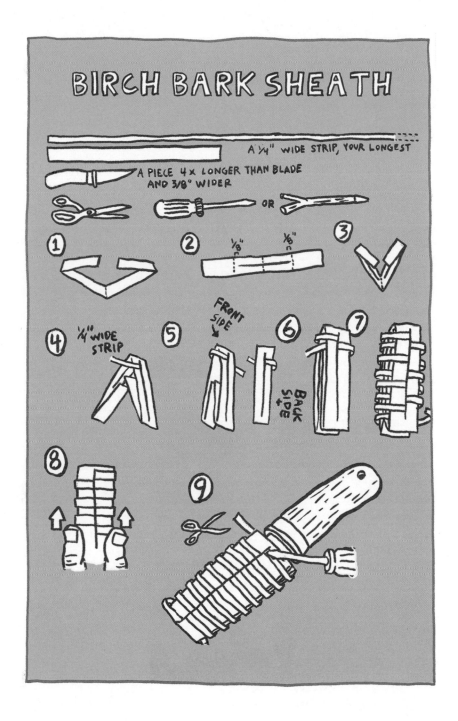

Vegetable oil (optional)

A board or a piece of cardboard to use as a cutting surface

A knife to be sheathed and used

Scissors (optional but handy)

A screwdriver or a stick with a flattened end (optional)

HOW TO DO IT

1. Make sure your birch bark is flexible enough to bend without cracking. You can take off a few layers to make it thinner if need be. Conditioning the bark strips by rubbing a little vegetable oil into them with a rag can make them more flexible and leather-like. Fold the wider strip in half and crease it on the fold. Then open up the strip and fold each end in to the creased middle line. Crease the folds.

2. Open it all back up, and with your knife, carefully make a slit down the middle of the middle two sections, keeping ⅛ inch back from the end creases.

Alternatively, flip out the inner folded pieces and keep the long piece folded in half, then, using scissors, cut both layers from the middle fold down to ⅛ inch before the next crease.

3. Fold the ends back into the middle and then fold the whole thing in half.

4. Slip the end of the ¼-inch weaver strip under the slit at the end of the sheath that is by the center fold.

5. Fold the weaver strip around to the back and over the top of the first side of the folded piece, then put it through the slit and under the second side of the folded piece, bringing it back around to the front.

6. As the weaver strip comes around to the front on a slight downward angle, it goes over the right side of the folded piece, through the slit, then under the left side of the folded piece and around to the back again, slipping under the first side through the slit and over the second side.

7. Continue in this manner, keeping to the under-over pattern on the front and back. Sometimes you'll be going over and over again or under and under again as you go from the front of the sheath to the back, but the under-over pattern as you are looking at the front and back is what matters (see the illustration).

8. Stop once in a while to tighten up the weave by pushing up on the cross pieces, making them as tight against each other as possible. If you run out of weaver strip, tuck the end under the slit and overlap a couple inches with a new piece of weaver before continuing on.

9. At the end, push everything up tight, fold it around the edge, and trim off the weaver, leaving just enough to slip it in the last slot on the side. If everything is super tight, a screwdriver or a stick with the end flattened can help open the space to stick the end of the weaver into.

10. Slide the sheath over your blade and make another, because now you're hooked!

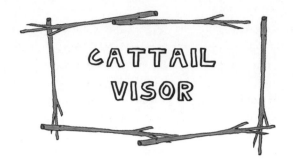

CATTAIL VISOR

MAYBE WHEN YOU STARTED OUT the sky was cloudy, or maybe you forgot to check your "ten essentials" list (page 64), or maybe you've just got a sudden hankerin' for some serious backwoods style. Whatever the case, it's a pretty simple task to whip up a cattail visor that will protect your face from the sun. With their big, brown, hotdog-like seed heads and the light, fluffy seeds that reside within, cattails are one of the most common and easily recognized plants in wet areas, which means the makings for your new visor should be simple to find.

STUFF YOU'LL NEED

Twenty long cattail leaves
(Yup, really, that's it!)

CATTAIL VISOR

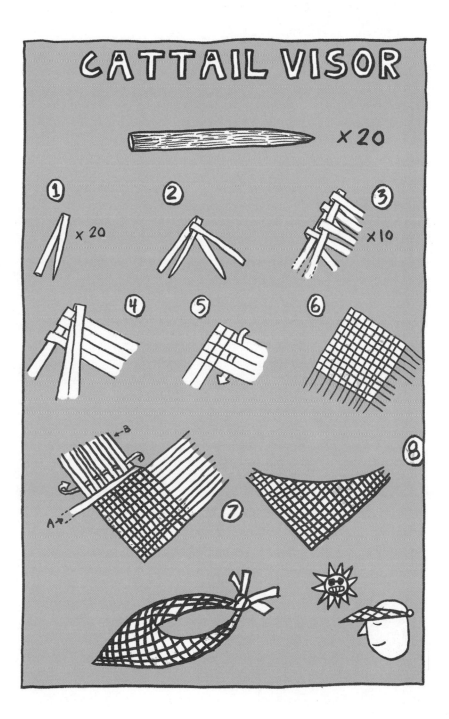

HOW TO DO IT

1. Fold all the cattail leaves in half.

2. Take two leaves and slip one side of one of them inside the fold of another to lock them together and make a corner.

3. Now take nine more leaves and, alternating whether the fold goes around the top or bottom of the first folded leaf, slip them through in the same manner next to one of the first leaves. At this point, you should have ten leaves folded around one leaf.

4. Pick up one of the remaining leaves and slip the fold around the leaf, perpendicular to the leaves you just inserted.

5. Using the two sides of the folded piece as one, go under and over, under and over all the leaves perpendicular to the piece you are weaving with. Each time you go under or over, make sure you are going under or over both sides of each folded piece.

6. Do the same weaving with the rest of the pieces to make a checker-board-like woven square with the ends of the cattails coming out of two sides.

7. Hold the weaving so the corner between the two sets of loose ends is facing you. Starting with the cattail on one side closest to the corner (A in the illustration), keep the top and bottom of the folded piece together and fold at a 45-degree angle so it lies parallel to the cattails it started out perpendicular to (B in the illustration). Weave it over and under, using the two pieces of all the folded cattails as one. Once you have woven that leaf out to the end, fold it around the last leaf and weave it back until it runs out.

8. Continue weaving four more leaves on that side, and do five going the other way. This should leave you with a visor-shaped weaving with five folded leaves sticking out right where you could twist them together and tie the visor around your head. Which is very convenient, because that's exactly what you're about to do!

BIRCH BARK CONTAINER

YOU MIGHT THINK that plastic and metal containers are superior to traditional storage vessels made of natural materials, but in this case the modern options fall way short. Paper birch, also known as white birch, is the best species for everything from containers to canoes because it has a strong, cardboard-like bark that is easy to cut, bend, and even sew. It keeps out moisture, maintains temperature, and boasts antibacterial properties that protect against rot. Native Americans discovered these things and put this material to a myriad of uses, including these folded containers that are easy to make, hold water, last a really long time, and literally grow on trees. It doesn't get much better than that.

Birch bark containers can be used for harvesting wild foods, transporting and holding water, and even cooking, but their primary traditional use was to gather maple sap, because they could be constructed quickly and were light and easy to distribute throughout the sugar bush (the stand of sugar maples used for sap collection). That said, feel free to put whatever you want in yours.

It's really, really important to harvest birch bark with care, or you'll do a lot of damage to the tree. It's so important that we wrote a whole sidebar on how to harvest correctly, so please, please read

that carefully before you harvest. A few other things you should know before you begin: Fresh bark can be used without any special preparation, but if you need to store bark before making your container, lay it flat and weight it down, or it will curl up tight. If you end up using stored bark, it'll need to be heated or exposed to very hot water to make it flexible again. Our advice: Do your best to use fresh bark. It's way easier.

Also, if the bark is really thick and hard to fold, you can peel several layers off the white, papery side. Even still, thicker pieces might need to be lightly scored with a dull point to facilitate folding. Finally, avoid bark that contains knots, or your container will leak. Oh, and you might want to practice with a piece of paper before using precious bark.

STUFF YOU'LL NEED

A sheet of birch bark 8 to 12 inches wide by whatever the diameter of the tree you harvested it from was

Twigs

A straight edge and pencil (helpful but not essential)

Something blunt to score fold lines with (a thin nail works well)

Four clothespins

HARVESTING PAPER BIRCH BARK

Sometimes it is possible to seek out areas where disturbance is planned for the near future, such as logging oper-
ations or land clearing. Another option is finding someone
who harvests firewood; one birch tree will provide you with
a ton of material, and you don't need to worry about dam-
aging a tree that's going to be burned as firewood anyway.

That said, it is possible to harvest bark from a live tree
without killing it, but it is a delicate procedure. The easiest
time to harvest bark is when the tree itself "gives up the
outer bark"; this happens from about mid-June to mid-July,
when the sap is rising and the bark is under tension because it has not yet adjusted to the internal expansion of
the wood. Try to find a medium-sized tree (maybe 8 to 10
inches across) with a straight section that's free of knots
and other blemishes.

The trunk of the tree consists of the bark, the cambium, and the wood pulp—you want the bark and *only* the
bark, which is dense and consists of many layers. Make
a shallow vertical cut (usually less than ¼-inch deep)
through the outer layers of bark, but *not* into the cambium.
Getting the right depth is *key* to ensuring the tree survives
over the long haul.

Once you've determined how deep to cut, make a vertical cut 8 to 12 inches long. Then, from each end of that
cut, make a short, horizontal cut. You should be able to
get your knife under a corner and gently lift the bark away
from the cambium. Use your hands to separate the rest of
the piece from the tree. If it is prime time, it will pop right
off; if not, you might have to try a little harder to slowly
work it off.

HOW TO DO IT

1. Clean up the outside of the bark by removing loose material. Then, using scissors or a knife, square up the rectangle. Use a straight edge and pencil if you are *that* kind of person, or eyeball it if you are *that* kind of person. Don't know which kind of person you are? Your friends and family do!

2. Very lightly, so as not to go through the bark, score lines onto the bark at the places where you'll be making your folds (as in the illustration). Scoring the bark is not absolutely necessary, unless your bark is on the thicker side and hard to fold up. You could just look at the illustration and pull the corners together and make a container with bowed sides instead of sharply folded-up sides.

3. Fold the sides up by pulling together the corners as at points A and B in the illustration. The triangular piece that sticks out as a result is then folded flat along the short side. Hold it down with a clothespin. Repeat with all four corners and set aside.

4. Make a small slotted hole in each folded-over corner near the top. Use a knife, a sharpened stick, a nail, whatever works.

5. Cut two flexible twigs a little longer than the space from hole to hole. Put a slight point on each end and flatten one side of each twig.

6. Fit one end of a twig into one hole, and then, flexing it slightly, poke the other end into the hole on the other corner as seen in the illustration.

7. Find something to carry in your new vessel; at the very least, be sure to eat your next meal from it.

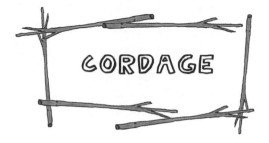

CORDAGE

QUICK QUIZ: How are string and toilet paper alike?

Quick answer: They're both one of those fundamental things that we take for granted until we need a piece (or two) and don't have it.

And like toilet paper, string is also one of those simple things that have stood the test of time. Adhesives, nails, and molded plastics have taken over some of the jobs string used to hold down, but until you transition your wardrobe to plastic, string is going to be a pretty big part of your life.

The exact date of the discovery of string, aka "cordage," is in question, but it's pretty likely that you have your Neanderthal relatives to thank for its invention. Of course, they didn't invent cordage just so you can cover your birthday suit; they had a half million other Neanderthal-ish tasks to accomplish, such as assembling nets to catch fish, making snares and bow strings for hunting game, attaching handles to tools, and lashing rafts. Sliced bread is pretty handy, but string is possibly the most useful invention in history.

Cordage is made from two or more strips of fibers that are twisted or plied together. It can be made from animal sources such as animal or human hair, hides, sinew, or gut, as well as from plant fiber. The Incas in South America were plant-fiber maniacs;

they built ships and made armor out of it. Their greatest weapon, the sling, was woven from plant fiber and could throw a projectile powerfully enough to break a steel sword (see "Shepherd's Sling" on page 118). They used string to communicate through an elaborate language of knots, and amazingly, they even used twisted grass and other vegetation to make bridges!

Native peoples of North America have always possessed a vast knowledge of cordage, as well. In fact, the basic methods of this ancient technology have remained relatively unchanged throughout the ages and across cultures.

The next time you find yourself without a piece of string when you need it, here's a little tutorial on how to make your own cordage from the plants around you.

HOW TO FIND AND PREPARE THE RIGHT PLANTS

Many plants across North America have fibers that are useful for cordage. A short list includes dogbane, milkweed, stinging nettle, cattails, cedar trees, and basswood trees. If you can't find plants to work with, an African grass called raffia is commercially available and carried at craft stores. It is also possible to use strips of almost any flexible material to practice with. Old jeans, T-shirts, and even plastic bags are all good options.

Dogbane and milkweed are easy plants to find and start with (see the sidebar on page 144). Find the dead stalks in late fall through winter, best after the first frost. Take care in harvesting, as the stalks are still attached underground to the living rhizome from which the new stalks will grow. The lower part of the stalk should be brittle enough that you can just snap it off. Discard the top branchy part and any pods still attached.

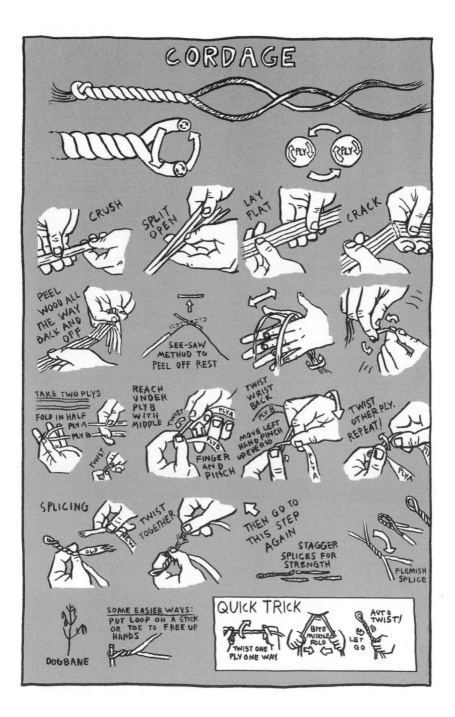

CORDAGE

CRUSH

SPLIT OPEN

LAY FLAT

CRACK

PEEL WOOD ALL THE WAY BACK AND OFF

SEE-SAW METHOD TO PEEL OFF REST

TAKE TWO PLYS

FOLD IN HALF

PLY A

PLY B

TWIST

REACH UNDER PLY B WITH MIDDLE

TWIST

PLY A

PLY B

FINGER AND PINCH

TWIST WRIST BACK

PLY B

MOVE LEFT HAND PINCH UP EVER TO

PLY A

TWIST OTHER PLY. REPEAT!

PLY A

SPLICING

TWIST TOGETHER

NEW

OLD

THEN GO TO THIS STEP AGAIN

STAGGER SPLICES FOR STRENGTH

FLEMISH SPLICE

DOGBANE

SOME EASIER WAYS: PUT LOOP ON A STICK OR TOE TO FREE UP HANDS

QUICK TRICK

TWIST ONE PLY ONE WAY

BITE MIDDLE FOLD

LET GO

AUTO TWIST!

To separate the bark (which you want) from the inner wood of the stem (which you don't want), follow these steps:

1. Crush the stalk down its length. Fingers usually work, or use a rock. A friend of ours uses the car door to crush a whole bundle at once!

2. Split open the stem by running a finger down a crack.

3. Lay it flat so the inner bark is split into four lengths.

4. Crack off a 2-inch section of the inner wood at the thick end and peel the pieces of wood off the bark from the top, back toward yourself.

5. Crack off the next 2 inches of wood and start to peel off back toward yourself. When the wood is about halfway peeled off, peel from the other side using a see-saw method to get the whole pieces off without removing a bunch of fiber with them.

6. Continue up the stalk, taking 2-inch pieces off at a time until you have clean ribbons of bark.

7. The ribbons will be covered in a flaky outer bark that you can remove by twirling them between the palms of your hands.

REVERSE-WRAP METHOD FOR MAKING CORDAGE

Of the many ways to make cordage, the reverse-wrap method is a good place to start. Basically, you'll be taking two bundles of fiber and twisting each of them individually in one direction and then twisting those two bundles together in the opposite direction (see the diagram at the top of the illustration).

HOW TO DO IT

1. Cordage can be made as thin as thread or as thick as rope. Gather a bundle of fibers a little bigger in diameter than what you want your finished cordage to be, and tie them together with an overhand knot at one end.

2. Divide the fibers into two equal bundles, then pinch the knot between the thumb and forefinger of your left hand (if you're a righty), keeping the two bundles separated into PLY A and PLY B with the loose ends sticking out to the right.

3. Use your right hand to twist PLY A away from you. As you twist, continue turning your wrist so you can grab PLY B between the forefinger and middle finger of that same hand.

4. Now, twist your right wrist back in the opposite direction, which reverses the position of the two plies, putting PLY B on top and PLY A on bottom.

5. Slide your left hand off the knot and over to the right, securing the new junction of the plies.

6. Release the two plies from your right hand and regrip the upper ply, now PLY B, with your thumb and forefinger.

7. Repeat this sequence over and over until one ply starts to get thinner. At this point, take a small amount of new fiber, lay it on top of the ply that is getting thinner, and begin using it as one. Make sure to keep the diameter of the cordage consistent and the splices staggered, to avoid ending up with weak spots.

8. Keep going until you have a piece the length you want. In the end you will have a piece of string many times the strength of the original strands. That said, it's probably a good idea to practice a bit before you make a bridge over a steep gorge.

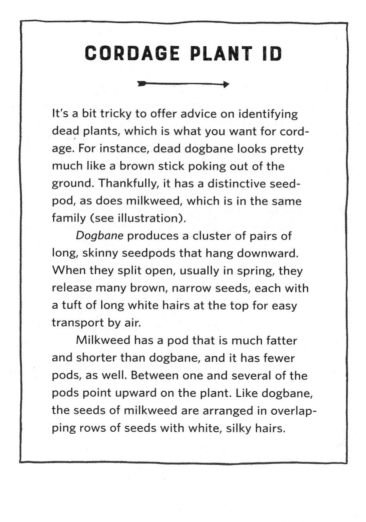

CORDAGE PLANT ID

It's a bit tricky to offer advice on identifying dead plants, which is what you want for cordage. For instance, dead dogbane looks pretty much like a brown stick poking out of the ground. Thankfully, it has a distinctive seedpod, as does milkweed, which is in the same family (see illustration).

Dogbane produces a cluster of pairs of long, skinny seedpods that hang downward. When they split open, usually in spring, they release many brown, narrow seeds, each with a tuft of long white hairs at the top for easy transport by air.

Milkweed has a pod that is much fatter and shorter than dogbane, and it has fewer pods, as well. Between one and several of the pods point upward on the plant. Like dogbane, the seeds of milkweed are arranged in overlapping rows of seeds with white, silky hairs.

LOG RAFT

AS THE INFAMOUS HUCKLEBERRY FINN once said, "There warn't no home like a raft, after all. Other places do seem so cramped up and smothery, but a raft don't. You feel mighty free and easy and comfortable on a raft."

Who doesn't want to feel mighty free and easy? If you do, it ain't too hard to build your own raft. Here's how.

STUFF YOU'LL NEED

Logs: You'll need six or more logs that are roughly 8 inches in diameter (but it's more important that they are all the same-ish thickness) and 6 or so feet long. You'll also need four logs that are strong but smaller in diameter; these should be an appropriate length to sandwich the bigger logs, as seen in the illustration.

Experiment with what floats best. Dry logs float better than green (or fresh), some species float better than others, and waterlogged logs don't float well at all. Standing dead trees that haven't been soaking up water on the ground are a good choice. Pine and cedar are examples of trees that are less dense and therefore more buoyant. More dense and they might float but not enough to keep you up out of the water and feeling mighty free and easy.

Rope: A good 30 feet should do it. Nylon will last longer. Rope sold as clothesline is a good diameter. P-cord (parachute cord) sold at hardware stores is lightweight, nylon, and super strong.

HOW TO DO IT

1. Set yourself and your materials up near the water, because few things in life are more ridiculous than dragging a raft across dry ground. Line up the big logs next to each other, alternating larger and smaller ends of each log if they taper significantly. Scrunch them together as tight as you can.

2. Put a smaller log perpendicularly on the top and bottom of the row at either end, as shown in the illustration.

3. Make a loop at one end of the rope with a bowline knot (see page 73). Wrap the rope loosely around all the logs, as shown in the illustration. Once the rope is in place, go back and tighten the whole thing, pulling out all the slack you can from the beginning to end. It can help to have an extra set of hands or to tie the loop end of the rope temporarily to the log.

4. When you get back to the loop, pass the end through the loop and then, pinching the free end tightly to the loop, use two half hitches (see page 74) to cinch it tight.

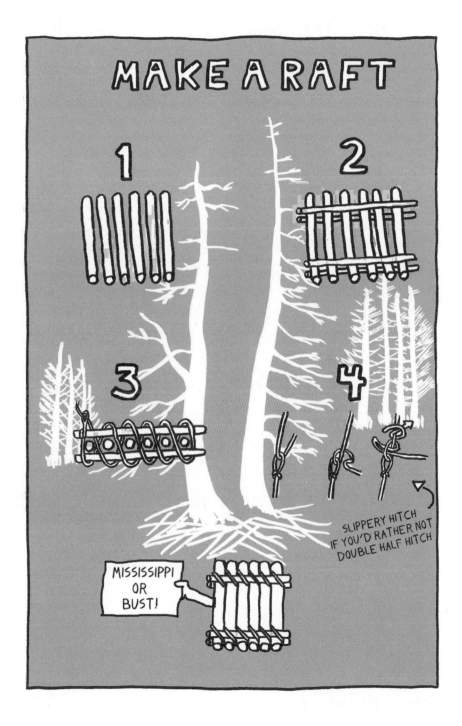

5. Rafts are poled, not paddled, so find yourself a likely pole. The exact length of your pole will depend on the depth of the water (you want the pole to touch bottom). The diameter should be determined by your grip size; you need it to be comfortable in your hands.

6. Try it out in shallow water at first. Assuming it floats, don't waste another second: Head straight to the Ole Mississippi and start polin' (don't forget your lifejacket!).

FELT HAT

FOR CENTURIES, PEOPLE AROUND THE WORLD have used wool felt for clothing, footwear, dwellings, rugs, and a variety of other textile needs. Felt is the oldest form of fabric known to humankind. Many years before people learned how to spin and weave yarn, they discovered the tendency for natural fibers from animal wool or fur to mat together when warm and damp, which developed into a technique known as wet felting.

Felt can only be made from certain types of fiber, including most fleeces from sheep or alpacas, as well as hair from Angora goats (mohair), Angora rabbits, and rodents such as beaver and muskrats. That's because these fibers are covered in tiny scales. Heat and moisture cause the scales to open, and agitation causes them to latch on to each other and become entangled. Soap helps the process by allowing the fibers to slide easily over one another.

Basically, wet felting is the process of using water, soap, and agitation to shrink and lock animal fibers together permanently, creating a denser, smooth fabric. If you put a barrier, or "resist," between layers so they don't felt together, you can make a three-dimensional object like a hat. Give it a shot!

STUFF YOU'LL NEED

Lid to a plastic storage tote (if you are doing this project inside)

Towels

A flexible tape measure or a piece of string and a ruler

Cardboard (thick is better than thin; corrugated works if you duct-tape the edges) or heavy-duty plastic to use as a resist

Scissors

Two pieces of bubble wrap, about 2 feet by 2 feet; you can tape pieces together

4 to 6 ounces of wool roving or raw wool in whatever color or colors you choose

Cheesecloth (available at hardware stores and some grocery stores or online) or a piece of screen or mosquito netting or the like

A squirt bottle (optional but handy)

Hot water

Soap (pretty much anything works, although people have all sorts of recommendations; we use liquid castile soap)

Newspaper or other material to stuff in the finished hat to hold its shape

HOW TO DO IT

1. Notice that this technique is called "wet" felting. This means that things get wet: definitely the hat you are making but probably also you and the floor. Set yourself up so as not to make too much of a mess. A warm day outside at a picnic table is optimum. If you need to do the felting inside, the lid to a plastic storage tote works great as a tray. You can also just layer a couple towels under the project.

2. Figure out the size of the resist by measuring your head with the tape measure or wrapping the string around your head and measuring the string. However you do it, figure out the circumference of your noggin. Cut the measurement in half since the wool wraps around both sides of the resist. Now add 30 percent to that measurement, since that is how much the wool is likely to shrink during felting.

3. Cut the cardboard or plastic in a hat shape with the bottom edge the length of the measurement you came to above. Make the dome part in proportion to the bottom edge, remembering that it will all shrink about 30 percent.

4. Put one piece of bubble wrap on your work surface (or in the lid) and lay the resist on top.

5. Begin pulling small tufts off your wool supply and use them to make a thin layer covering the resist and extending 1½ to 2 inches beyond all the edges except the bottom one, with all the fibers going horizontally. Add another thin layer of wool tufts with all the fibers going vertically. Repeat with another horizontal layer and another vertical layer, totaling four thin layers.

6. Put the cheesecloth (or other netting) over the wool. Use a squirt bottle or your hands to sprinkle hot water over the cheesecloth-covered wool. Put on a few drops of soap. Gently press your hands flat on the cheesecloth and begin working in the water. Just move your hands back and forth a little so you don't displace the fibers. All you are trying to do is thoroughly wet the wool; it should take a minute at most.

7. Peel back the cheesecloth. Put the other piece of bubble wrap over the wool, and then, sandwiching the two pieces of bubble wrap between your two hands, flip the whole thing over. Take off the top piece of bubble wrap and fold the extra 1½ to 2 inches of wool over the top of the resist. This extra wool will connect the two sides of your hat. Smooth it down flat.

8. Layer more wool on this side in the same way as you did the other side: four thin layers, alternating the horizontal and vertical directions of the fibers. Again, make sure you extend 1½ to 2 inches over the edge of the top part of the hat, leaving the bottom edge even with the resist.

9. Cover the wool with cheesecloth. Sprinkle a little hot water and a few drops of soap onto the cheesecloth-covered wool and work them in.

10. Put the bubble wrap on top and flip to the first side. Fold the wet fringe of wool over the edge and smooth it down. Cover with netting.

11. Gently massage the wool with your hands, pressing gently from the outside edge toward the center. You don't want a big soapy mess, but your hands should slide easily over the cheesecloth. If they don't, use a little more soap and hot water. The massage pressure should be light at first. Go for about 5 minutes, flip to the other side, and work that side for 5 minutes.

12. Flip back and forth, applying more pressure as the surfaces start to harden. When the wool turns to firm fabric, take out the resist. This could take 30 to 45 minutes.

13. Put some soap on your hands and some hot water on the hat, and with your hands sandwiching the hat—one hand on the outside and one hand on the inside—vigorously rub the fabric all over, paying extra attention to the seam where the two sides came together and the bottom edge that is the hole for your head. This edge will not be straight, but don't worry, that can be fixed later.

14. Put the hat on a piece of bubble wrap with the opening down, squirt on some more hot water and roll them up together on the tray. Roll it back and forth over and over, maybe twenty-five times or more. Unroll and turn the hat so the opening is to the side, then squirt on more hot water and roll it up again. Back and forth, back and forth, twenty-five more times. Unroll and flip the hat over, then roll it again. Unroll, turn the hat 90 degrees, and roll it again. Whatever direction you roll or rub in, the hat will shrink in that direction, so keep switching it up.

15. With a sharp pair of scissors cut the brim even. Use hot soapy water to rub the raw edges you just cut until they are hard and no longer fuzzy.

16. Run the hat under hot water in the sink, add a little soap, and keep rubbing and rolling it in your hands. Alternate with cold water to shock the fibers.

17. Rinse and ring the hat out, and try it on periodically to see if you like the fit. The brim can be folded up or not. Keep felting until it is the right size. Thoroughly rinse all the soap out, wring out all the water you can, stuff it with newspaper to keep the shape, and let it dry. A warm place overnight usually does the trick, but it can take longer.

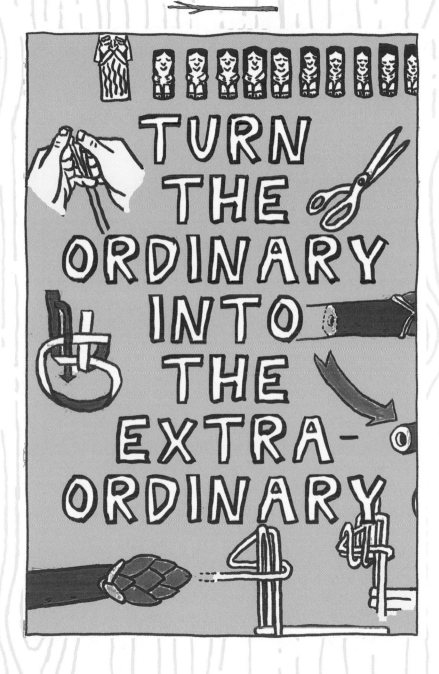

PART FOUR

TURN THE ORDINARY INTO THE EXTRA-ORDINARY

TURN WILLOW BRANCHES INTO A DEER

FILE THIS ONE UNDER "Cool Projects That Look Way Harder Than They Actually Are" (aka "CPTLWHTTAA"). Archeologists have found split-willow figures across the Southwest, some dating back several thousand years, to a time before smartphones ruled the universe. It's believed these figures were first used in hunting rituals and later as children's toys, but since no one who was there is around to talk about it, no one really knows. So if you make one, you can do whatever you want with yours, and in a few thousand years (or maybe a few less), no one will know what the heck its purpose was.

STUFF YOU'LL NEED

One slender (pencil-thickness or less) green (meaning fresh, not the color) willow shoot, at least 30 inches long. It should not have any branches growing off it.

HOW TO DO IT

1. If the willow has leaves, strip them off. Cut an inch or so off the tip end. Using your fingernails (unless you're in the habit of biting them), slowly split the shoot from the cut end, as shown in the first illustration. If the split becomes uneven, with one half bigger than the other, bend the fatter side more sharply as you work. This will bring the split back to the center of the shoot. Split all the way down but *stop* 1½ inches from the butt end.

2. Bend the willow twig at a 90-degree angle at the point where you stopped splitting. This forms the back leg of the deer.

3. Leave about 2 inches for the back, holding the two parts of the split willow together, then bend only the piece that is on top down 90 degrees to form the front leg. Make it the same length as the back leg; then bend that same piece of willow back on itself to make the piece stick straight up, forming the neck. This might all sound a bit confusing, so be sure to look at the illustrations as you work.

4. Now, take the other half of the back bone, which is sticking straight out, and use it to make the body wider by wrapping it around the front and back legs again and again until all of it is wrapped. Then tuck the end of the twig back inside the body to secure it in place. (If it seems like too much, just snip the extra off before tucking it in.)

5. Take the neck twig that is sticking straight up. About 1½ inches up from the body, bend it back on itself and bring the end down on one side of the body and under the belly and back up the other side, basically wrapping it around the body to lock things in place.

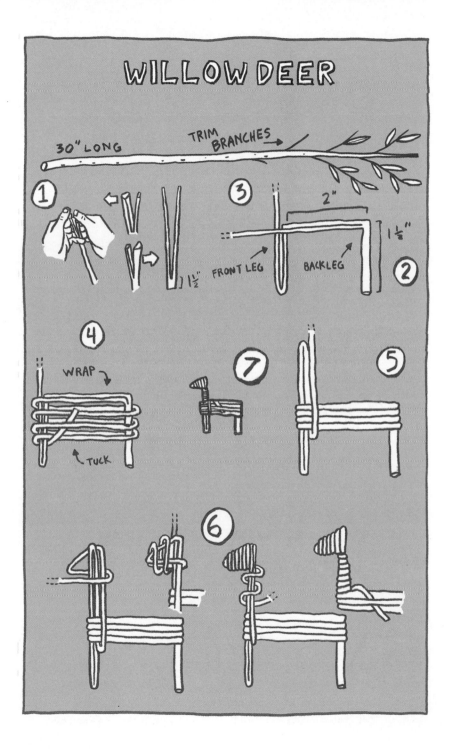

6. The piece should now be pointing straight up again. Use it to form the head by bending it over the folded neck piece and shaping it into a backward number 4. It is a little tricky to hold everything together while you work, but after you shape the head, wrap the twig around the neck and back to the nose. From the nose, wrap around the head again and again until the whole head is wrapped. Wrap the neck with the remaining length and tuck the end under part of the wrap to secure it in place.

7. We're guessing it might've taken you a while to make your first deer, and that's OK: the first one is always the hardest and slowest. As you make more, you'll get way faster and will learn to adjust the proportions.

MAKE A WHISTLE
FROM A STICK

HERE'S A QUESTION that's probably been keeping you up nights: What makes a whistle whistle? You'll be glad to know we've got the answer: A whistle whistles when a stream of air directed at the edge of an opening in a chamber oscillates (this is a fancy word for "kinda bounces off either side of the edge like a fluttering flag").

To create just such a chamber in a stick, you first have to remove the sticks' innards, which sounds sorta icky and difficult, but is actually a piece of cake, especially if you choose the right tree at the right time of year. The right tree is willow, and the right time of year is spring, when the layer of cells between the bark and the wood fiber is growing rapidly and is very fragile. This means you can crush this in-between cambium layer by gently tapping on the bark with a heavy object, allowing the outer bark to slip off, revealing the slick, white, "clean as a whistle" (sorry, we couldn't help ourselves) wood surface.

STUFF YOU'LL NEED

A knife and saw. (Just a knife will do it, but a saw makes things a little easier.)

A straight section of a live willow branch that is about a half inch thick with smooth bark. (Actually, this works with a bunch of different trees, so don't be afraid to experiment, but willow works consistently well.)

HOW TO DO IT

1. Cut a section of the branch about 4 inches long—making sure it doesn't have any knots or branches sticking out.

2. About ¾ inch from the end, score through the bark all the way around the stick.

3. Now you need to loosen the bark by tapping the large area of the stick, leaving the ¾-inch piece alone. Tap with your knife handle (blade in sheath, of course, unless you're fond of bleeding) or a small hammer. You need to tap hard enough to loosen the bark but not so hard you crack it. It may take 5 or 10 minutes of tapping. Hold on to the ¾-inch piece and try twisting the bigger piece to see if it is loose enough to slide around, but leave it on the stick for now.

4. Use a saw to cut off a piece of the end of the long side on a diagonal (see the illustration). This forms the mouthpiece.

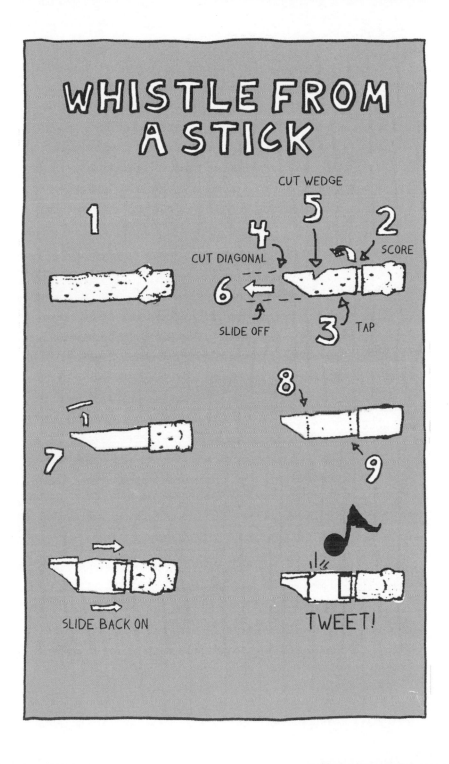

5. Next, cut a wedge out of the top of the whistle (see the illustration) by making a cut perpendicular to the branch closest to the pointed end and a diagonal cut up to meet it. You can use a saw for this part—or maybe a knife to get through the bark cleanly and then a saw to go through the wood.

6. Carefully slide the bark off the branch.

7. To let air into the whistle, you need to shave a bit off the pointed end of just the wood part, $\frac{1}{16}$ to $\frac{1}{8}$ inch, parallel to the line of the stick (see the illustration).

8. Now, cut the triangle end of the wood piece entirely off. A saw would be easiest, but a knife will work if you carefully roll the piece around under the knife until it cuts through.

9. Take that triangular "plug" (actually called a "fipple plug," which is obviously one of those cool terms you'll want to hang on to so you can blow some minds at a later date) and set it back in the bark mouthpiece the same way it was originally.

10. Cut about 2 inches off the other wood piece and plug up the other end with it.

11. Blow!

CREATE A ONE-OF-A-KIND JOURNAL

THE COOL THING ABOUT JOURNALS is that they can be anything you want them to be. You can write about the classmate you're secretly in love with, or why your parents are so dumb it makes your head hurt, or you can just doodle pictures of your pet iguana. The other cool thing about journals is that the journal itself can be as unique as what it contains. Here's how to make your own.

The first thing to do is decide on the cover material. It can be pretty much anything you want, though you probably want something that's a bit thicker and tougher than the inner pages. You might try birch bark, fabric, leather, heavy-weight paper, even cardboard. The only limit is your imagination. Well, that, and the laws of physics.

YOU'LL ALSO NEED

Ten sheets of 8½- by 11-inch paper

Scissors

A pencil

A ruler

Thread

A needle

An awl or some other pointy tool

Cover material cut to 6 by 10 inches

HOW TO DO IT

1. Cut the 8½-by 11-inch sheets of paper in half horizontally.

2. Make four piles of paper with five half sheets in each.

3. Fold each pile in half horizontally and stack the folded piles on top of each other.

4. Place a mark along the spine of your stack ½ inch in from each end and then 1½ inches in from those marks, for a total of four marks.

5. Fold the 6- by 10-inch cover material around the stack of piles and open it back up, holding the stack in place. Make marks on the inside of the cover next to the marks on the spine, $\frac{1}{16}$ inch out from the edge of the stack. Make three more marks to the left of each of those marks, $\frac{1}{16}$ inch apart. Poke a hole at each of the marks with the awl.

6. Open each folded pile and make holes with an awl at each mark.

7. Cut a length of strong thread about 10 inches long. Thread the needle and put a knot in the end. From the inside of one folded pile, poke the needle through the bottom hole and into the corresponding hole in the cover, and pull it out the right side of the cover. Stick the needle back through the cover's second hole up, through the next hole up in the folded pile, and pull it through to the inside. Poke the needle in the third hole up and through to the right side of the cover, then in the last hole in the line on the cover, bringing the needle back to the inside of the fold. Tie off the thread.

8. Repeat this running stitch for each of the four folded piles.

9. Now, bust out your pen and start inking up your new journal!

YO, MAKE A YO-YO!

MAKING YOUR OWN YO-YO is one of the simplest, most satisfying skills in this book. Here's how to make it happen.

STUFF YOU'LL NEED

A bow saw

A curved stick (as a brace to help hold the bow saw)

A straight branch that has the diameter of the desired yo-yo (about 3 inches, or the thickness of your wrist, is good). The branch should be approximately 2 feet long so you have enough material to grip safely as you complete the steps in "How to Do It."

A wood rasp (if you don't have one, ask someone who works with wood regularly)

A length of string or twine that's about as long as the distance from your waist to the ground

HOW TO DO IT

1. Take a bow saw and place it vertically, sandwiched between your knees. Put a curved stick across the bottom of the saw where it touches the ground and step on both sides of the stick; this will hold the saw steady. Now pinch the saw handle between your knees. This might feel a little awkward at first, but it's a great technique for cutting wood in the bush, because it allows you to put your entire body weight into sawing.

2. Using up-and-down sawing motions with hands gripping your yo-yo branch on either side of the saw, cut almost all the way through the wood but leave an axle that's approximately $\frac{3}{8}$ inch connecting the two pieces. Try to make the axle centered and as evenly round as possible. That said, don't stress: It doesn't have to be perfect. And it's only a yo-yo!

3. Take the curved edge of a wood rasp and work the cut into an even valley all around.

4. Saw 1 inch away from your cut on either side of the branch. You should now have your yo-yo piece. You can clean it up with sandpaper. Or not.

5. Tie one end of your measured string around the axle, then tie a loop in the other end that's just big enough to stick your favorite yo-yoing finger through. Wind it up and get to it.

MAKE A VIKING GAME OUT OF STICKS

LEGEND HAS IT THAT the Scandinavian lawn game *kubb* (pronounced "koob") was played over a thousand years ago by the Vikings. Some say the game pieces were made from the bones of their enemies, which is pretty intense if you think about it. Which is maybe a good reason to not think about it. For your game, we suggest using logs.

The rules of kubb are simple and open to wide interpretation or variation depending on the skills, ages, and imaginations of the participants. It involves skill and strategy, and be warned: it's addictive!

If you don't have access to logs, you can get wood from a home center or lumberyard, in the rough dimensions of the logs specified. Use an 8-foot 4-inch by 4-inch piece for the king and kubbs and 2-inch and 1-inch dowel for the batons and field markers. (Just don't get the pressure-treated stuff. Pressure-treated lumber is full of chemicals, and the pieces of this game will be handled a lot.)

THE PIECES

Dimensions can be approximate.

One 12-inch piece of a 4-inch-diameter log (the king)

Ten 6-inch pieces of a 3-inch-diameter log (the kubbs)

Six 12-inch pieces of a 2-inch-diameter log (the batons)

Six 8-inch pieces of a 1-inch-diameter log (the field markers)

TOOLS

Handsaw

Pencil and tape measure or ruler (optional)

Knife (optional)

1. Prop the logs up on something so the end you are cutting off is hanging over the edge.

2. Measure the length and mark it with a pencil or just eyeball it.

3. Keeping the hand that is holding the log well back from the saw (unless you like the Viking idea of using bone), cut the pieces. You can make this as refined or rustic as you want, but do make sure that the cuts for the king and kubbs are straight so they will stand up on their ends and not topple over.

RUSTIC OPTION

Read the directions below and start winging chunks of wood around.

REFINED OPTIONS

Sand everything smooth.

Carve or paint cool designs on the kubbs.

Carve a crown on the king and paint designs or a face.

Carve points on the field markers for ease of pushing them into the ground.

Make a carrying case.

DIRECTIONS

Two to twelve players can play at once. A game can take anywhere from 20 minutes to several hours to play.

THE GOAL

Be the first team to knock down all your kubbs and then the king. Or if the other team knocks down the king before their kubbs, you win!

THE SETUP

Mark off a 16- by 26-foot field with the markers at the corners. Don't be too precise; just pace it off and call it good. Stand the king in the center and evenly spread five kubbs along each baseline.

THE GAME

Team 1 starts by standing behind its baseline and throwing all its batons at the kubbs on the opposite baseline, trying to knock them down. The batons must be thrown underhand and must travel straight or end over end. They cannot be thrown horizontally or sidearm.

When Team 1 is finished, Team 2 stands at their baseline and throws any knocked-down kubbs back into the far half of the field (the king is at the centerline). These become known as "field kubbs." Team 2 has two chances to throw each kubb into the opposite half of the field. If they throw the kubb out of bounds twice in a row, the offending kubb is placed 6 inches behind the king.

Once all the field kubbs have been thrown, Team 1 stands them up. If a kubb was thrown into the field and it hit another field kubb, the kubbs are stacked on top of each other. There is no limit to how many kubbs can be stacked in this way.

Team 2 then must knock down all the field kubbs before throwing at the baseline kubbs. Any baseline kubbs that are knocked down before the field kubbs do not count and are stood back up.

When Team 2 has taken its six throws, Team 1 picks up any knocked down kubbs (both field and baseline) and throws them back into the opposite half of the field for Team 1 to stand up.

If at any time a team does not knock down all the field kubbs in their opponents' half of the field, the other team is allowed to move up to the kubb closest to the centerline and throw batons from that new line.

Play continues in this way. The game is won by the team that knocks over all the field and baseline kubbs in their opponents' half of the field and on the baseline and then knocks over the king. All attempts on the king must be from the baseline. However, if a team knocks down the king prior to knocking down all the kubbs, that team immediately loses the game. Which means it's time to start another!

MAKE A BIRCH BARK RING

WHETHER YOU MAKE ONE FOR YOURSELF, or to give to a friend or sweetie, birch bark rings are super cool. Also cool is that you can whip one up in about 5 minutes flat . . . though we recommend keeping that part to yourself. Just peel a skinny piece of birch bark and follow the steps in the illustration.

BIRCH BARK RING

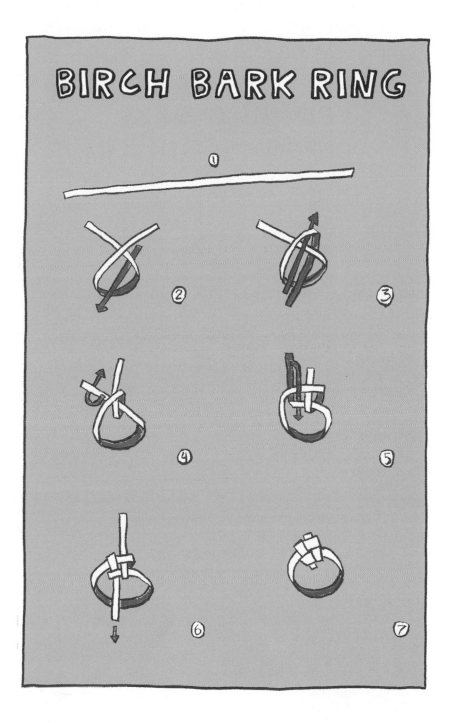

CREATE YOUR OWN BEADS FROM TWIGS

WHETHER YOU'RE LOOKING FOR a super-easy and exceptionally cool gift, or something unique to wear as a symbol of a memory or event, or just a fun way to pass time in the woods with friends, twig beads are your answer. They're really quick and simple to make in their basic form, but they can also be as intricate as you want to make them.

Twig beads are possible because of a substance called "pith," which is the soft, spongy cellular material in the center of tree branches. The job of pith is to store and transport nutrients throughout the plant, and it's generally present only in the young growth of trees. Some species, such as elder, sumac, ash, and willow, have particularly soft pith, which makes them easier to hollow out or poke a hole through.

STUFF YOU'LL NEED

Pruners

Pithy, smallish diameter branches (about ¼ to ½ inch)

A poking tool to hollow out the beads (stiff wire or a small-diameter nail works best)

String or thin wire

A knife

HOW TO DO IT

1. Cut branches into lengths that will be workable as beads.

2. Poke your tool into the end of the bead pieces and rotate it round to hollow out the soft pith.

3. When you get a pile of beads, feed them onto a piece of string or thin wire to the length you want for a bracelet, necklace, anklet, zipper pull, or whatever, and tie or twist it off.

4. Be all proud of yourself.

5. See the sidebar for design ideas, or make up your own.

There are more ways to personalize your beads than there are branches in the world to make beads out of. Here are a few ideas to get you started.

▶ Using a knife, cut designs in the outer bark to reveal the lighter inner wood. Dots, squiggles, stripes, or *x*'s can look cool, or you can create your own personal symbols.

───────

▶ Cut in initials, names, or words.

───────

▶ Scrape all the bark off every other one.

▶ Cut your beads into different lengths or from different diameter branches.

───────

▶ Have each person in your group make a bunch of the same design and trade them around so you all end up with matching bracelets.

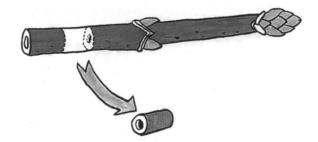

TURN AN ACORN CAP INTO A WHISTLE

WARNING: AN ACORN WHISTLE IS SERIOUSLY ear-piercing. Unless you want to strike fear into the hearts of pets and family members alike, do *not* practice using one indoors. For this very reason, it makes a fantastic emergency whistle.

STUFF YOU'LL NEED

You guessed it: an acorn cap! The bigger the cap, the easier it is to learn on; the smaller the cap, the louder the whistle. You decide.

HOW TO DO IT

1. Mentally draw a Y on the inside of the cap, dividing it into three pie slices with the intersection being a little above center, making the top slice a bit smaller than the others.

2. Grasp the cap with your thumbs and index fingers, hiding the bottom two pieces of the pie with your thumbs, tops bent and rotated out in a Y shape.

3. Purse your lips and blow hard. The knuckles of your thumbs should rest right between your lips. Play around a little. The angle of the cap might need to be changed so part of the air stream curls around inside the cap and the rest goes over the top edge. You also might need to vary the size of the top triangle (the part that is visible between your thumbs).

4. Learning to play one of these simple whistles takes a bit of practice. There's no real secret other than to just keep working at it until all the neighborhood cats are scattering in fear.

TURN TURKEY FEATHERS INTO A KITE (THAT ACTUALLY FLIES)

MAKING A KITE WITH TURKEY FEATHERS is one of those projects that scores really high on the effort-to-fun ratio. To improve on that ratio even more, gather a group of friends, have everyone make their own kites, and have a fly-off.

STUFF YOU'LL NEED

Six wild turkey wing feathers. (If you can't find them in the wild, ask a turkey hunter or look on eBay or Etsy online.) You need three from one wing and three from the other.

Scissors or a knife

Scotch tape

Two 4-inch lengths of dogbane. (You can also use drinking straws—the heavier, the better.)

Two 4-foot lengths of surveyor's flagging

Twine or string

A pool of fishing line. (If the line is connected to a fishing pole and reel, even better!)

HOW TO DO IT

1. On two of the feathers, clip the end of the shaft so that the shafts of two other feathers can be pushed into them. The two feathers you clip need to be from the same wing, and the two feathers you insert need to be from the other; this orientation is important for proper flight (just ask any bird)!

2. Insert the feather and wrap the joint in tape.

3. Using an X pattern, lash the feathers to the lengths of dogbane or straws with twine as shown in the illustration. The two lengths of dogbane should be almost, but not quite, parallel—with the rear tips slightly farther apart than the front tips. The front pair of feathers should be directly at the front tips of the dogbane, while the back pair should be located about an inch forward of the rear tips.

4. Insert the remaining two feathers into the pithy end of the dogbane.

5. Tie a piece of twine to the center of each side of the rectangle formed by the dogbane and the pairs of feathers. The pieces hanging down should be about 4 inches each. Now tie the loose ends of these together into a knot.

6. Tie one end of your fishing line to the knot.

7. Tie a length of surveyor's tape to the end of each tail feather. This helps with stability.

8. Wait for the breeze to pick up, head for an open space, and let 'er fly!

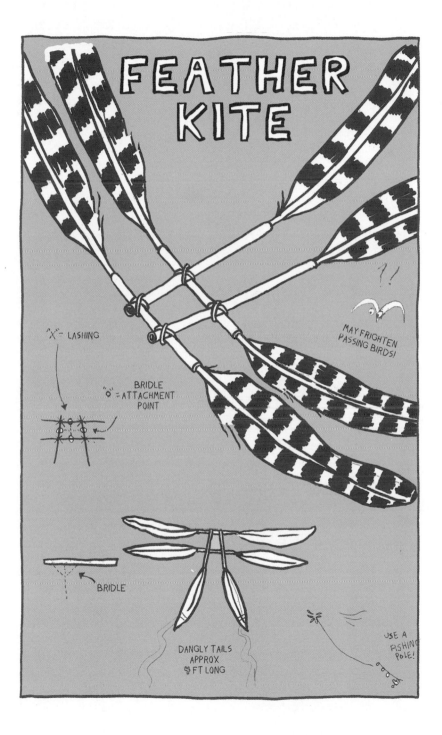

ACKNOWLEDGMENTS

➤───────────→

BEN AND PENNY would like to first thank their sons, Fin and Rye, whose boundless energy and curiosity have taught them more than they ever knew possible and without whom this book would not exist. They would also like to thank those who have shared so generously their skills and wisdom, including many they will never know and a handful that they do. They are particularly grateful to Erik Gillard and Nate Johnson for their generosity of wisdom, time, friendship, and poems. Thanks to Luke Boushee for his wonderful illustrations, for being such a pleasure to work with, and, most importantly, his friendship. Finally, thanks to Erik Gillard for his written contributions and to Barry Wyman for contributing "Using Bird Language to Track in Real Time."

Luke would like to thank his mother for encouraging him to draw, as well as all the human and nonhuman teachers who inspire him in nature connection. And thanks to Ben and Penny for the opportunity to collaborate on this book!